A COMPILATION OF EMOTIONS

YOU ARE SIGNIFICANT

D . S - R

A COMPILATION OF EMOTIONS
YOU ARE SIGNIFICANT

iUniverse books may be ordered through booksellers or by contacting:

iUniverse
1663 Liberty Drive
Bloomington, IN 47403
www.iuniverse.com
844-349-9409

ISBN: 978-1-6632-2875-8 (sc)
ISBN: 978-1-6632-2876-5 (e)

Print information available on the last page.

iUniverse rev. date: 05/11/2022

CONTENTS

Some of the content in this book can be found in my first book.

INTRODUCTION

Good Morning Jesus my Savior
Good Morning Mary my Mother
Keep me from sins today
Keep me from sins forever
Oh Lord I love thee with all my heart
Let me begin this day with a virtuous start
I thank you for all you've done for me
Bless all the people and my family
Help me that I will always love you
Everything pleasing to you, I will do

2003

I am eternally grateful to the creator of the universe who provides me with the thoughts and words to express myself so they can be understood by people of all races, ages and social status. I am beholden to HIM for the strength he lavishes upon me so that I can continue to overcome obstacles, breach barriers and persevere in my position despite any negativity.

I know that the raging fiery effects, not only from the bombs of war, but from the negative "isms" that plague society, will eventually be extinguished.

I believe that one day, we will witness the disappearance of those "isms" which present barriers that prevent any semblance of a society, in which everyone can experience a decent, meaningful, fruitful, and fulfilling life.

How can we create this change? Let's introduce a new positive "ism": "SIGNIFICANISM".

I would like to extend heartfelt gratitude to my brother who agreed to write the foreward for my book. He painted a picture as seen from the eyes and soul of the patriarch of the family.

I am also grateful to Joyce Bales, an avid reader, who made me realize how little I read. She would ask me "Have you read such and such"? Even though I was familiar with the name of the author, I would have to say "No". She encouraged me to share my poems, and would always, say "You have a way with words".

Thank you, Glen Easter, the Great and Powerful, for your wisdom, suggestions, and constant curiosity about the progress of this book. His question was "Did you call Oprah yet"?

I would like to thank John Torres, Retired First Sergeant, for his steady support and inquiries, every time he saw me. His greetings were always, "How's that book coming along"? When am I going to see you on Oprah"?

I would like to thank Mr. Dexter Ward for his technological instructions, support, and well wishes for the success of this book, and the expectation that it will be a best seller.

The completion of this book would not be possible without the contributors. I would like to extend my gratitude to the students, soldiers and instructors, who were willing to share their experiences, or provide information, which added more substance to the project.

I would like to express my deepest appreciation to Mayor Jose Segarra, for writing the Afterword. Mayor Segarra continues to support the English as a Second Language Program, as strongly as he supports the Killeen community. He is able to relate to all the students, both military and civilian. He attends the Certifcate Presentation Events in the classroom and City Hall, and speaks to the students and their spouses about the importance of learning English. He also addresses their role as it applies to their rights and obligations in society, Civics, and his role and responsibilities as the Mayor.

If I am able to lift one person's self-esteem or open someone's eyes to the existing possibilities, then I will have realized my dream. Do you know your secret gift or strength? Find it and use it.

FOREWORD

There is a universal saying, which, when paraphrased, states that if you wish to help someone it is better to show them how to fish rather than give them a fish.

It therefore came as no surprise when I learnt my sister was writing this book. She has always been a very gifted individual of many talents filled with diverse forms of expression. Her military journalistic career has evolved into a noteworthy passion for teaching people, from all walks of life and various countries, who need encouraging and uplifting.

The book explores the roles that spirituality plays in our lives as they undoubtedly did in her vast experience. The central theme throughout, also evidenced in her poems and quotations, is the positive message of overcoming obstacles and creating opportunities for a better life. It provides an avenue for the reader to assess his or her own true identity in navigating the environment within the adaptive process so as to maximize their potential. This is a critical part of human development particularly for persons finding themselves in a "different" culture.

The author draws from her marinade of multilingual capability, as well as her profound empathy for immigrants, to guide them through the myriad of changes they face from day to day. This is effectively achieved through her obsession with words that translate directly to the spirit of the reader and therefore serves to give better understanding on the path to fulfillment and success. A must read for everyone, this book furnishes the inspiration to motivate anyone.

D.R.S

"Aller Anfang ist schwer" is a German expression that means all beginnings are difficult. This certainly holds true for people who immigrate to the United States and have to understand both the language and the culture. Education is often the key to this understanding, and people who seek it will make their beginning at their new home less difficult.

When I first came to the United States from Europe, I thought I had a good grasp of the language. I had started taking English classes in 5th grade, and I was now 22. However, the experience was quite a culture shock. My first job in the United States was at a college, and when I started taking courses there, I learned quickly that my dictionary was my best friend. I always carried it in my purse. Even then, pronunciation presented problems. Once, when I found myself standing at the cash register with a "rope," and my friend had a "robe," I learned the big differences that one subtle sound can make.

I also had interesting experiences with American foods. The first time I went to a restaurant in Killeen with my friends, I was very surprised when the waiter brought me pieces of meat coated with some kind of weird crust. Where was the chicken I ordered? In Germany we usually eat rotisserie chicken, but this "fried chicken" looked and tasted nothing like it. An excellent way to express your native culture is by sharing traditional dishes with people from different cultures.

Later, when we finished our meal, my friend paid and we immediately left the restaurant. I was wondering why we were in such a hurry and thought perhaps we were going somewhere else as a surprise for me, but to my disappointment we just went home. In German restaurants, dinners are very big and drawn out, with long conversations that usually last for hours. Needless to say, my learning curve about American language and culture was great.

Many immigrants experience similar language barriers and cultural differences when they arrive in the New World. My advice is to start taking English-as-A Second Language courses as soon as you arrive, like these students who are sharing their experiences with you, in this book. English-as-Second Language courses cover basic grammar, reading and writing, and cultural studies, but moreover they give students the confidence to explore the world around them and embrace change. Every time I attend an end-of-school year celebration, English-as-A Second Language students show pride in their accomplishments and gratitude, about having learned so much in the program.

I believe the important part is to explore and appreciate your new country and still hold on to some of the traditions of your home country. All these experiences enrich us as individuals, and they also make American culture what it is. This book will provide you with a diverse array of reflections and will take you on an international journey.

Tina J. Ady, Ph.D,

I AM IN LOVE! YES! IN LOVE!

I fell in love at a very early age. I fell in love with languages and words- little words, big words, English words and foreign words. Before I had two digits to my age, curiosity pertaining to languages and vocabulary piqued and invaded my mind.

My mother and grandmother used to communicate, particularly when they did not want me to be privy to their dialogue, in a language I did not understand. Not being able to understand placed me in a state of invisibility. So I embarked on a journey to familiarize myself with the language so that I could be a part of the conversation. Imagine the looks on their faces when they realized that I understood what they were saying.

Around the age of eleven, I was madly in love with French words, Spanish words, and Latin words. I had the golden opportunity to study these languages at St. Francois Girls' College, the only Girls' Government Secondary School, in the twin-island Republic. According to Pasha Lalla-Seecheran, Principal Secondary (Ag), the education system in Trinidad and Tobago has become more inclusive over the years. The staff has increased from 40 in 1989 to 59 presently, including 4 Heads and 4 Deans. The student population has increased from about 500 to 740. She said, "The school has always had a strong Language Department, dating back to 1962, and continue to offer French and Spanish, which remain compulsory". I quickly realized that once you put words together correctly, with each word in its proper place and form, it was magical. I'm in love with writing and editing.

In Military Journalism School, we were told to write for an eighth grade audience. I asked myself, what about all those "big" words I learnt? My answer? I did not have to use them, but if I came in contact with sesquipedalians, I would be able to understand what they meant.

CHAPTER 1

Although Egyptian and Sumerian civilizations studied writing about 3,000 years B.C, some of the functions then are still the same today. It was used to record things and tell stories. The Sumerians and the Egyptians had different forms of picture writing. Many of the sculptures of the Sumerian art displayed in the Lourdes Museum, Paris, have writing of some form. The Sumerians advanced from simple pictograph to graphic writing that represented a concept. Then writing was developed into a tool that could communicate ideas. To foster understanding, communication is necessary.

To initiate communication, words, verbally or written, are essential. Although our brain can store a quadrillion bytes of information, as time goes by, sometimes retention can be somewhat difficult. Some people say "Write it down", and that is exactly what I do.

I write not for money or status, but because it is an extension of my soul. Writing gives me solace. It extracts bottled-up emotions. I experience an emotion, I write; I observe something, I write; I am in a pensive mood, I write. When thoughts gain access to my mind, I reach for my best friend and put pen or pencil to paper. This can happen anywhere and anytime at home, on a bus, in a taxi or any hour of the day or night. I write not from assumption or hearsay, but from observation and experience.

I can teach anywhere, in a shack, an empty space, the woods, as long as I have the instrument to disseminate the information to the students who have the three Ds DESIRE, DETERMINATION and DEDICATION to inhale and digest it. External dialogue is very powerful. Internal dialogue, if not more powerful, once transferred to the page, can have a profound effect, because people get to actually see the words and imagine.

Imagination can take you anywhere. If someone is inspired to any degree by what I write, it is well worth it. Words, written or spoken are creative instruments that can have significant effects.

There is something in my soul that forms a need to put my thoughts into words, and not only put them on paper, but transmit them verbally to my students. When HE wanted to create the world, HE spoke. Words are creative forces that can bring into existence, things that never existed before.

It is an absolute joy when I am with my students. I thoroughly love and am ecstatic about what I do. I get an overwhelming sense of satisfaction that I do not ever want to lose. I am always in a receptive mood when it comes to information, whether it is information with which I agree or disagree. I too, am a student when I am teaching, because I learn so much from each one of them every day. I use the knowledge I gain, not only to accomplish my goals, but to help others so that they can accomplish theirs. There is no limit to the love I have for what I do.

A portion of this book is directed at some of my students, immigrants from every corner of the world, who feel comfortable enough to share some of their personal goals, dreams, tragedies, setbacks and experiences with me; the ones who find the trust and strength to allow me to be the ear and receptacle for their "baggage", and the ones who tolerate the ridicule and threats they encounter from others. Not being a licensed professional psychologist, therapist etcetera, I am not in a position to give advice, thus, I do not.

However, if my words of encouragement, based on my personal experience, could inspire and uplift someone, it would be spiritually satisfying.

During World war 11, the United States again recognized the importance of foreign languages and and foreign language education. Individuals and educators started to welcome other languages, got an appreciation and showed encouragement to learn English through ESL education. According to an Adult ESL Specialist at the Center for Applied Linguistics, Adult basic education has been federally funded since the adult Education Act of 1966 and the 1970 amendments to that legislation that expanded educational services to include ESL and citizenship. We know that some of the benefits after receiving citizenship are:

*The right to vote": You will be able to become informed and understand the rights, laws and the political system of the United States.

*Obtain a U.S passport.

*Petition for members of your family to come to the U.S.

*Apply for federal jobs etc.: Being bi-lingual can increase the chances of obtaining a better-paying job.

CIVICS is now a requirement in our ESL classes, and students are provided with instruction that consists of more than rote memorization of facts and figures.

VISITS

For example, students become actively involved by visiting City hall and getting to know the community and city leaders. This way, they receive first-hand information about the role and responsibilities of the leaders.

ESL programs exist nationwide and internationally. Some incur a fee and some do not. Sometimes, depending on the state, the Adult Education budgets are cut across local districts where Beginning, Intermediate and Advanced level ESL classes are normally conducted.

It is quite evident, that in order for immigrants or anyone for that matter to learn a language, resources must be available. Here at the Adult education program, qualified instructors and teachers, coupled with experienced administrative personnel ensure students are adequately schooled, provided with the necessary resources and the state's goals are attained.

Living in the United States and not being able to speak English can sometimes be a condescending experience in some circumstances.

VOLUNTEERING

Volunteering is an essential part to our being, accomplishments and identity. There is a natural sense of happiness and satisfaction.

When we volunteer, we give our time, effort and knowledge, and in some cases sacrifices are made, to help others. We also give our HEARTS. Some students volunteer at schools, churches and organizations, and they support local fairs and food drives. They do this in spite of their limited English skills.

The language barrier can affect and at times prohibit relationships. Some immigrants are reluctant to integrate, but assumptions should not automatically be made that one is stupid because one does not speak another person's language.

Students share stories about the discouragement and frustration that seep in and become factors that impede the accomplishment of their goals. There can be a lingering presence of animosity, which creates a distance resulting in the lack of any type of communication.

While visiting Prague several years ago, I greeted an elderly gentleman in Russian. His reaction was unexpected. He returned the greeting, got on his knees, kissed my hand and shouted "Gavareete Pa Roo ski" (You speak Russian)!

No matter what nationality, some people exude a certain degree of excitement and pleasure when a person from another country speaks or even attempts to speak their language. It shows there was definitely an effort to fill the communication gap.

I know of immigrant students who were reluctant to integrate and have actually returned to their countries out of frustration.

Others decided to stay and immerse themselves into the learning process by first studying ESL (English as a second Language).

The students acknowledged are some of many who fit the latter, and they have the number one ingredient necessary for success-DESIRE.

Ninety eight percent of my students are affiliated with the military. Like many others, no matter which nationality, they are faced with several issues that could prevent them from attending classes regularly or even at all. Cases in point:

TRANSPORTATION: Many times, there is one vehicle, and that poses a problem. Additionally, the student might not have a driver's license yet. So, students get together and organize rides, or travel to the post with their husbands (for Physical Training) and wait until class begins.

DEPLOYMENT/TRAINING: This can be lengthy and unpredictable and sometimes for both soldiers and spouses, this will prevent them from attending classes.

CHILD CARE: Sometimes, the family cannot afford child care and does not initially know anyone who would assist them. Therefore, they would enroll in night classes, and this way, their husbands would take on the role as primary caregivers for those few hours.

JOBS: Students do get jobs commensurate with their level of knowledge of English, and at times the hours can conflict with the class schedules. Therefore, they work out a schedule where they can attend classes in the morning and work in the evening or vice versa.

APPOINTMENTS: (Immigration/legal/medical). These can occur very often in certain cases. Students take the initiative to try to rearrange dates (very difficult) or make up classes whenever possible.

Despite all these issues, reasons, challenges, these students find solutions and make the sacrifices necessary to achieve their goals.

One student, with a nursing degree from her country, found time to volunteer in a hospital while she was attending classes. She felt that in addition to her classes, working around people who spoke English would also help. After volunteering for about eight months, she applied for a position in a local hospital and was hired. She still attends ESL classes.

Another student, who did not want to discontinue her classes, sought advice from her instructor as to how she could continue her classes, because her shift was changed and hours increased. Discussions were held, and classes and schedules were arranged to accommodate her situation.

Students with little or no education are able to spell the word "Antidisestablishmentarianism". I do not expect them to know how to spell it when I present the challenge the first day of class. However, I tell them they would be able to spell it before they leave the class. For some, it takes weeks, months or a matter of days.

One student, sixty-two years old, who never had any schooling in her country, wrote the word on the board after three days. I stared with surprise as she counted each letter to verify the accuracy. She said she wrote it many times because she was DETERMINED to spell it.

After taking her son to school one day, another student's car broke down. I mention this because I know of students who would have contacted me (same day or next day) to say they could not attend class because the car broke down.

This student, a punctual student, was late that day. Why?

Yes. She walked to class. She walked! Nowadays, we drive everywhere; even to the store on the corner or the mailbox at the end of the block. She walked! She was late, but she was present.

Yet another student, with a third grade education from her native country, exhibits the qualities and actions of some students who are studying for a degree. Her inability to read to her daughter and assist her with her homework triggered her interest in taking ESL classes.

Another example of the desire to learn is the student whose son had an appointment. Before taking him to the appointment, she stopped by the classroom with her son to turn in her homework, collect some notes and pick up the day's assignment.

Yet another example of the "yearn to learn" is the group of students who chose to attend class four days, instead of two, because they felt that they would learn more- The Faithful Four.

One soldier always found the time (time is something we can find) to attend class before or after an appointment, after training and after duty. The soldiers studying ESL are acutely aware of the importance of learning English. They realize that effective communication and comprehension are vital in the execution of not only the daily duties but the overall accomplishment of the mission. Even more aware are the noncommissioned and commanders who afford them the opportunity to fulfil this requirement without interrupting training.

Kudos to these students! They make sacrifices, follow instructions, participate in class and demonstrate the three D's consistently. There are more examples, and they all are applauded for their efforts. Those who decide to stay in America believe they can acquire the language skills and customs necessary to participate and contribute in some measure to their families, communities and society.

On the other hand, I know of students who have tried to destroy character and careers, with complaints for a variety of reasons. They were either becounseled, suspended, did not get to the Advanced level, or dropped from classes because of their failure to follow instructions or adhere to the rules that are set in place.set in place.

To those students, I say "adjust your moral compass". Anger and retaliation are dangerous NOUNS to employ when things do not go the way you would like. Try to do better. You can.

Those students should understand that they cannot do things or have things their way all the time, especially in an institution or organization when specific rules, regulations and policies have been established.

There are systems that are created to address those situations. Such systems are deemed to be professional and therefore should not make decisions from a personal viewpoint. We all can do better.

Some students have degrees from their countries, and they seem to believe that they know everything when they attend ESL classes. In some cases, they think they know more than the administration/ teacher/instructor. Well, they might, in another area, but not in the subject at hand. They shouldn't be there if they did.

There will always be someone who knows more than we do-always. If there are classmates whose listening comprehension, grammar skills, or communication skills seem to be better than yours, sieze that opportunity to learn from them. There is no place for jealousy.

Unfortunately, in some instances, when some students realize that they don't know as much as they thought they did, frustration and embarrassment surface, which slows or shuts down the learning process.

Again, no matter what nationality, some people exude a certain degree of excitement and pleasure when someone from another country speaks or even attempts to speak their language. It shows that there was definitely an effort fill the communication gap.

Learning another language might not be mandatory, but it is definitely an asset. Maybe if we took some time to learn and understand a language and learn about each other, effective communication and comprehension will certainly surface. This will foster some understanding between cultures, and in addition to the obvious benefits, perhaps, just perhaps, the world can be a better place. The possibility exists.

To my students-all my students, current and former: Introduce yourself to you; know who you are, not only on the outside but also on the inside. If you do not like yourself, you will not like anyone else-not superficially- but internally. Do you like your inner self? If we look inside and do not like what we see, we have the power to change. But we cannot change what we will not confront. You are great!

Surround yourself with greatness; with knowledgeable people who will not hesitate to share. The people with whom you surround yourself can have immense influence on who you become, depending on the quantity and quality of your strength. Greatness is not how great you shine, but how great you make other people shine.

What you do is what matters. Do good things for those who are not able to do for themselves. It does not have to be something monetary or monumental. One of the most special things you can give to someone is your time (time is something we can find). Take some time to listen-not hear-listen.

One morning on my way to work, a soldier walked past me and said good morning. I answered and asked "How are you?" He replied "I'm good"-an expected response nowadays.

But his tone was not "good", so I stopped and repeated the question with emphasis on the "are".

This soldier began to unleash his emotions and talked about his Army experience, personal affairs and the direction he felt his life was headed. I listened. I offered no advice, but I talked with him about the time when I had some similar experiences and felt lost and stagnant in the Army. I shared what I did to change my situation. He said "Thank you for listening." We both listened to each other.

You do not have to move mountains. Little things done with love and earnestness can make a big difference in other people's lives. Be encouraged-do not be discouraged. There are times when you may feel stagnant and imprisoned in a strange place because of the language barrier and nationality. When I first came to this country, I felt lost and alone, and I had to create a path to find my way. It took DESIRE, DETERMINATION and DEDICATION all the way.

We should look at people because of their inherent qualities, or lack of, not because of their nationality.

People who frown upon your inability to speak English fail to realize that this is your second language. There are those who have problems with English being their first language. When it comes to vocabulary, pronunciation and grammar etc. you may be a little rough around the edges. Remember, so are diamonds. Lack of employment, absence of family, financial and health problems, can only compound the situation. But with the right attitude-of FAITH, situations will change.

Be famished for FAITH. We must establish a spiritual connection where there is no room for any doubt whatsoever. Our FAITH must be steadfast. We also have to stop and really think. If we ponder before we decide, respond instead of react, the outcome might be different. Sometimes our problems and circumstances might be miniscule in comparison to others, but they are still our problems and need to be addressed. If you have never faced or encountered adversity, you have not lived.

Once you analyze, understand and recognize your weaknesses and strengths, you can truly accept yourself and pursue your passion. Work on your weaknesses and release your strengths. Everything you need to achieve your goal or accomplish what you are called to do is already inside of you.

If your goal is to stay at home, focus on your family and be the best mother, wife and person you can be, then do so.

If we have no goals or passion, then we are not complete. If we close our minds, then we prevent the possibility for growth and grace. You have a treasure trove of information waiting to be unleashed. Believe it and act on it. The DESIRE in your soul will allow you to begin and continue to do whatever you enjoy doing, and that DESIRE will get stronger.

One time, before I wrote my first book, I asked myself, "Can I do this?" Well, I answered my own question. I wanted to, believed that I could, so I did. Again, the three Ds were present. Some things are just meant to be, and when you find that "thing" that ignites the fire in your belly no one can take it away from you.

CHAPTER 2

Are you afraid of failure? No need to be. Failure is another opportunity for greater success.

Once I was on a nighttime land navigation course and I got LOST. I thought I had failed the course, but I remembered they taught us how to shoot a back azimuth. So I used my compass and was able to complete the course.

As in life, sometimes when we LOSE our way, we need to use our moral compass and try to get back on course.

When others say you can't, you say you can. One year, I decided to run a marathon. A couple of people tried to dissuade me, saying I was not trained or it was too long, so forth and so on.

I was not trying to set a record or anything like that. I enjoyed running, and I wanted to see if I could run 26.2 miles. I was determined, so I did it. It took me several hours, but I did it. The three Ds were in place--- DESIRE, DETERMINATION, and DEDICATION.

I remember when I crossed the finish line the huge crowd had already dispersed except for a few officials handing out medals and t-shirts. I ran past them in a daze. After the race, a couple of co-workers taunted me in jest with quips such as "Got lost"? "Took a break"? "We thought you changed your mind……", but in my mind, I thought, "Mission accomplished".

It did not matter how long it took; I got there. Silent excitement! Life's journeys are sometimes like marathons- challenging.

Do not worry about your foes and fears. You have the ability to respond and overcome challenges that confront you. Knowledge gained is the result of failure. We were created for a specific purpose-one that only we can fulfill. Sometimes failure can cause you to re-center yourself and your priorities, which can result in success.

Everyone, at some time, is faced with waves of criticism, condemnation and inferiority complexes.

You can change that. You can be anything and everything at any time. Again, many people have become successful and influential in some shape or form, despite countless setbacks and obstacles. So can you.

Your similar struggles and setbacks enable you to relate and empathize with others who have or are encountering the same. You can be that pillar of strength for someone and cause a tremendous change in that person's life. Your presence and position have already been chosen and assigned to you.

You cannot make bad things go away by denying their existence, but if you acknowledge, confront and deal with them, they will cease to exist. We crave answers immediately, but we must remember that everything happens for a reason, and that reason might not be apparent instantly.

Sometimes we have to stop complaining about what we do not have, and rejoice in what we do have. Try not to always be dissatisfied with yourself and life. Sometimes we have to delve into our past to repair the present and prepare for the future. Revisit the past for a while.

Do not stay too long; just long enough to relate, compare and decide. Of course willingness to improve is understandable, but continuous, prolonged dissatisfaction is nonproductive.

Take time to examine your life; an unexamined life is probably not produtive. Decide why you are here and why you do what you do. The acknowledgment of any situation suggests change is in the future. We know that language is powerful therefore we should use words laden with positivity not negativity. An aspiring outlook on life can set the wheels in motion for a new beginning.

Always pursue your dreams, because HE would not put the ideas in your head if HE did not think you could realize them. "You do not always have to BE the best, but you should always DO YOUR BEST" D.S-R. Again, do not stifle your potential. Unlock the door to your potential. Try not to become too complacent or settle for mediocrity. HE has the final say.

Recognize that we are not the only ones in pain, drowning or floating in an ocean of obstacles. Ask HIM for help, not just for you but for others around you. It takes a lot to care about others more than what you care about yourself.

Do not wait for others to encourage you. Do not rely on people's approval to define your worth or values. Some are intentionally cruel and may spew words of discouragement, but you have to encourage yourself. The people with whom you surround yourself can have a direct influence on your outcome. The greatest force is HIM. Go to HIM for your value and worth. Strength is not always physical, because it can come from within.

Whether you take baby steps or giant steps, the aim is to get there, to that place in your life where you feel grateful, grounded, satisfied and significant. DARE TO BE SIGNIFICANT IN SOME WAY. Again, do not worry about your foes and fears. You have the ability to respond and overcome challenges that confront you. Knowledge gained is the result of failure. IN THE RACE FOR KNOWLEDGE, THERE IS NO FINISH LINE. Have a voracious appetite for knowledge. We were created for a specific purpose-one that only we can fulfill.

I believe that success is sacred and subjective. If your dream is to own a home, have a job that you enjoy and raise a family, and you have reached that point despite crippling circumstances, then you are successful. Many people have become successful and influential in some shape or form despite countless setbacks and obstacles. So can you.

Do not stifle your potential. Unlock the door to your potential. Try not to become too complacent and settle for mediocrity. HE has the final say. Recognize that we are not the only ones in pain, drowning or floating in an ocean of obstacles. Ask HIM for help, not just for you but for others around you. It takes a lot to care about others more than what you care about yourself.

Fear, weakness and anger are factors that can silence your voice. Just as barriers pop up in life, you can set up barriers to prevent these factors from invading your mind. Don't react-respond. Speak up and muster the strength to ignite that fighting spirit that lays dormant in your soul.

Most people have been hurt at some point in life. Do not let the hurt overcome you and lead the way. When you let it go, it feels as though a burden has been lifted off your shoulder. Remember, you cannot make bad things go away by denying their existence, but if you acknowledge, confront and deal with them, they will cease to exist.

I believe we should use the bad moments we have experienced and turn them into teachable moments. This way we can prevent them from happening to someone else or us again.We crave answers immediately, but we must remember that everything happens for a reason, but that reason might not be apparent instantly.

CHAPTER 3

Some have lost their true being and place more emphasis on how they look as opposed to who they are. Some live in a materialistic world where success is deemed by possessions and money. But you can be rich also-with CHARACTER. Your character is developed through tough times. There are some things no one can take away from you FAITH, KNOWLEDGE and CHARACTER.

If you only focus on your external as opposed to your internal, your CHARACTER loses its place.

Some people do things for rewards and recognition. If we live our lives that way, we might live a disappointing life. I believe we should do things out of desire and because it is the right thing to do. DO THE RIGHT THING EVEN WHEN NO ONE IS LOOKING.

There are times when people may try to "box you in", or place you on the bottom rung, maybe because of your background, heritage, lack of finances or lack of education. Yes, we all have choices and preferences, but our choices and preferences should not result in favoritism.

You have to believe in yourself even when no one else believes in you. You also have to believe in someone greater, to be able to do that. Others may pretend to support you in your endeavours, but will take great pleasure in your demise if you do not succeed. Pray for them. Do not let anyone limit your career aspirations.

Dismiss the negative thoughts they sprinkle around you, because there is a force inside of you that is undeniable. Always keep the FAITH and TRUST because if HE did not think you could handle the obstacles placed in front of you, they would not appear before you.

One day I will do something significant for one person

or thousands. I don't know when, where and how, but I know why. I believe I was chosen to make a difference. HE is good-not sometimes, but all the time. He is AMAZING.

Only you can control what you do. One action can catapult you into the right direction. You do not have to be famous, rich or prominent to make a difference in someone's life. That action may not be monumental in society's eyes, but certainly life changing in that person's eyes. You can make a difference in someone's life.

Create a vision for your future. The difference between today and your future is information. If you do not learn anything new today, tomorrow will be just the same. So read, listen and observe. Your future is in your discoveries.

Plan a path and follow it. It may seem like a labyrinth, but just keep reminding yourself of what is at the end of the labyrinth. Find a sense of purpose that is paramount in your life. If you have a solid center, you will be able to control "YOU".

Sometimes, events in your life may not materialize the way you expect, and you think you have failed or fallen. There is absolutely nothing wrong with failure or falling, but there is something wrong with not getting back up.

Many people experience failures, in school, at work and throughout their lives, but we simply have to keep trying.

These words and thoughts are not only directed at those who might be desperately struggling or struggling to catch up. They are for the ones who feel lost, perplexed and discouraged. They are for the ones who are on the first or the last lap. They are also for those who believe they have "run the race" and are at their finish line. Never stop learning! Never stop growing! It is up to you to maintain that fighting spirit and persevere. Wake up, stand up, speak up, and never give up!

There is a chest of possibilities at your fingertips. So, if the possibilities exist, why not explore? Although you may not have a degree, a home or a family, you possess talents and gifts that can influence the outcome of your life and others.

You should also be aware of, and in tune with those who tend to prejudge you because of your nationality.

One summer, we were conducting registration for summer classes. Some students were inquiring where they should go and they were directed to me. A new employee at the site looked at me and said "Where you from?" Notice the absence of the verb "to be".

I answered and she remarked with a smirk, "And you teaching English", a pattern. I responded with a gentle "Yes Ma'am". I was not mad; anger is a wasted emotion that encourages illogical thinking; just sad. I was saddened by her ignorance. Anyone who knows the history of Trinidad and Tobago would know that despite the multilingual diversity, the principal language is English-Speak English, which was initially based on a standard of British English, having been under British rule until 1962.

Sometimes we use humour to mask our ignorance, when it could be used to gain knowledge. Ignorance looms large, but we can reduce the size by seeking knowledge. Ignorance is not necessarily a bad thing. It is when we make assumptions based on our ignorance, it becomes questionable. Those who have experience will know. Those who don't-won't. Knowledge and experience are the results of failure, and we fall so that we can rise-higher. I would rather have moments of significance than a lifetime of some of society's norms.

We all can and should try to do better.

Note: Some lines are intentionally repeated for emphasis.

CHAPTER 4

I would like to particularly thank those students, and there are many, who have acknowledged my assistance in their endeavour to learn and improve their English. There are so many that have "made my day". The following is one of several examples in the book. One evening I was waiting for the bus outside a building which was closed. A car drove by, slowed down, and continued to drive ahead.

A few minutes later a lady came out of the building, greeted me, and said "Would you like to come inside?" It turned out it was a former student who now worked in the building. Her eight-year-old son was with her, and we talked for a while. After all the pleasantries, the bus came. Her son offered to help me with my bags and in the process, he said, "You were my Mom's English teacher"? I answered yes, and he said "You did a great job". Oh! My! It couldn't get any better than that. No amount of money or awards could measure up to the feeling of satisfaction and motivation I experienced at that moment.

There are quite a number of former students who still call, text or stop by the classroom to say hello and "check on me". So when I had one such visit, of course I was happy to see the student.

In early March, when COVID intruded our lives, one of my former students from Africa stopped by the classroom. He asked me if I had gloves, masks and sanitizer. I did not. He told me that those items were not available in stores, and we needed to go to the Post Exchange right away to purchase them. At that moment, I became acutely aware of the seriousness of the situation.

Another student from Iran patterns the same concern. She calls me often to find out if I need gloves and masks and volunteers to bring some to my home. As a matter of fact, she called yesterday, June 17, 2020, and made the same offer.

Yet another student from Puerto Rico echoes the same disquietude when we speak about life after ESL. The conversation always ends with "Remember teacher, if you need anything or need to go somewhere, let me know".

Concern from my students is always refreshing and appreciated. Concern from my former students during COVID is especially satisfying.

In this book, I talk about issues on a broad spectrum, in general terms. In my third book "Barriers Beyond Borders", students and I will share our personal struggles and circumstances, we have encountered, that will change, have changed or became turning points in our lives.

INSTRUCTOR HEADS SOUTH

She's packed up her rain stick and her steel drum. "Island Girl" is headed south. But wherever she goes she will be "home." After more than five years as a journalism instructor at the Defense Information School at Fort Benjamin Harrison, Ind. and Fort Meade, Md., she is headed south to Big Country to work for "America's First Team," the 1st Cavalry Division at Fort Hood.

"I remember when she got here," said Mike Gose, a fellow instructor who also worked with her as a volunteer at a local radio station, in a reading program, for the blind in Indiana. "Man, what a voice. She could tell me to eat kah- kah, and I probably would. Her voice is so smooth. It's mesmerizing". Perhaps what makes Dianna feel at home is her ability to communicate in a number of languages.

Pamela Smith, who was stationed with Dianna in Berlin, Germany, said she remembers her being able to communicate with anyone. "If a Frei University student from Africa got on the bus in Berlin-Kakuna Tatizo. In a German restaurant-Kein Problem. At the closing of the (Russian) checkpoints-Da, Konyechna! Spanish? No hay problema.? Oh yeah. Francais? Pas de problem. And of course English. She is truly amazing."

Five years plus has provided ample time for her to endear herself to her co-workers, both military and civilian. Bob Diller, the senior journalism instructor, refers to her as "Island Girl" when he plays his Caribbean music CDs, and said that he will miss her Trinidadian rebuttals. "There's something about the way she says "Tomotto that makes me go weak in the knees."

Smith said Dianna is an inspiration to her, both personally and professionally. In any given situation, she conducts herself as a cultured, but courteous professional. "As the Non-commissioned Officer in Charge, Public Affairs Office, (in Berlin) Dianna was in charge of weekly training sessions. One week during training, she was using a flip chart to detail the proper way to camouflage the face.

About 15 minutes into class, she started talking about how to camouflage shadow areas on the face. She did not look at the chart. The soldiers in the room were all smiling and chuckling. "Finally she looked at the chart and discovered a picture of a scantily clad lady taped over the camouflage drawing. Realizing she'd been set up, she handled the situation coolly and calmly. She squealed and then ran out of the room, red in the face. I've never seen her so embarrassed. She is, above all else, a lady."

Lady or not, she is not above running to catch a bus. "(In Berlin) she told me about the bus system as soon as I arrived," Smith said. "She helped me memorize the times and bus numbers.

The public transportation system in Berlin is really great. Just one problem: The drivers didn't stop for long. Before there was ever a Forrest Gump, there was Dianna, yelling, 'Run, Pam, run! We can still catch that bus," Smith recalls. "We were always running after buses. Army PT 'ain't got nothing' on running after the bus."

Smith said she values her friendship with Dianna, "She's my mentor," she said. "She worked with me side by side. She has always been there when I needed help, both personally and professionally. Truthfully though, I got tired of chasing those buses."

As a Multi-Level English as a Second language Instructor, it is my desire and responsibility to impart the knowledge I have acquired through inquisitiveness, education and experience to you. As students, it is your responsibility to receive, process, digest, retain and add that information to the knowledge that you already possess, so you can progress, blossom and soar to extreme heights to then help others.

Es war einmal

You don't have to sleep in a cardboard box, under a bridge, or in a corner on the streets to be homeless. You could be in a subway "waiting for a train", that you never board. You could be in a telephone booth, with the phone to your ear, talking to no one.

You could be riding the bus and never ring the bell or press the button. Or, you could just be sitting in a coffee shop for hours "nursing" a cup of tea, wishing you had a key to a place you could call home, hoping for a place you could lay your head in the absence of a bed. HE is good!

POEMS BY THE AUTHOR

Humeur Pensive

Sitting in the solace of my abode-alone, not lonely
Contemplating on a mixture of memories
Asking questions, some answered, some unanswered
Those answered fill the void of the once unknown
Fear of the unknown is overcome with the acceptance of reality
Optimism, Pessimism, Realism? You decide.

Verdad

Negative truth is often dismissed
Positive truth is always
acknowledged
We query, we ask why?
Why not?

Things happen for a reason
Matters not the time nor season
Bad experiences are never wasted
They can enhance your life
because they were tasted

Schritte zum Erfolg

Her demure, petite appearance
Contradicts her vast experience
Knowledge and ambition
Set the stage for her current position

She has excelled over the years
Always one step ahead of her peers
She listens to both sides and is fair and just
Which in any organization, these qualities are a must

Staff concerns are not only responsibilities
They are on her list of priorities
Always finds time for one-on-one
In the end, gets the jobs done

Un Pilar de Nubes

Gazing upward to the sky
Moving objects zooming by
Smiling, reminiscing, about the past
Covered by a blanket so vast

Grey ones, white ones, under a sea of blue
Seemingly looking directly at you
Temporarily hovering above
Imagine! Protection and love

Despido

My inner drive shall never subside
Emotions exist I can't seem to hide
Some written, others spoken
At times even broken

I must be prepared
So the latter can be repaired
Be brave enough to explore
Strong enough to endure

Dismiss fear at the intrusion of strife
If not I'll be afraid for the rest of my life
It might take weeks, months or years
But, in the end, there will be no more fears

Luz en el Horizonte

As long as there is light,
I will write
Although I can write
in the night,

In a park
In the dark
On a train
In the rain

On the bus
No fuss
No pain,
It's never in vain

Musikalische Worte

Notes speak to musicians
Words elicit visions
Visions of what can be
Deciphering between possibility and reality

Mi Madre

Mothers are so dear to us
On Mother's day we make a fuss
I want the world to know you see
How much my Mother means to me

She cared for me for oh so long
She taught me what was right and wrong
She taught me at an early age
Have no regrets ~ just turn the page

A world's out there for you to explore
Find the key ~open the door
And when life's troubles get you down
Stand tall, give praise and stay strong

Though she's not here physically, in my heart
Through God, she's with me
Loved her then ~ I love her now
Stand up MUMMY ~ take a bow.

My mother was a formidable woman with a strength that gushed from her being. She never attended college, but she was one of the most intelligent people I knew. She was highly articulate and exceptionally smart. Her tenacious spirit and her quest for knowledge were immeasurable. She had a voracious appetite for reading; each time I saw her, she was working, cooking or reading. She surrounded herself with wise and knowledgeable people, some of whom possessed the same character traits she did. Subsequently, she used the knowledge and wisdom she gained to assist and uplift her children and those who were in need. No. She never won any Grammys or trophies, but her consistent efforts and actions, prompted the small community in which we lived to introduce an award titled "Mother of the Year", which she earned. -an ordinary person, doing extraordinary things.

Pater Meus

His life was surrounded by clefs
and measures
To him these were some of his greatest treasures
He possessed knowledge of which he was aware
And was always willing and eager to share

Undeterred by life's barriers and strifes
He continued to mentor throughout his life
Coupled with an extraordinary musical dexterity
He had this uncanny ability to be funny

There was always a minute or two for a joke
Despite the seriousness he placed on his work
He studied pieces by Beethoven and Mozart
And when he played or conducted
He did so from his heart

The first musician to conduct a steel orchestra for the Queen
Truly an honor, if you know what I mean
When the encores echoed throughout the crowd
At those moments, I was especially proud

Proud of what he strived to be
Proud of what he meant to me.

Amis ou Connaissances?

The bell doesn't ring:
There's no knocking on the door
I suspect it's because I have no more to give
So I guess I'll go ahead and continue to live

But it's not quite living
Seems more like existing
At times "Friends" appear
They pretend to hear

Once they know the situation
They take a back seat position
Sometimes I feel like taking a dive
But a voice tells me to go ahead and thrive

I listen to the voice and put my trust
Because, I do have a friend – in Jesus.

2012

D.S-R

Amikoj

A friend is someone who:
Listens without judging
Offers without being asked
Supports sans excuses
Cares without limitations
Shares without expectations
Forgives without hesitation
Criticizes without condemnation
Prays for and with you

QUOTATIONS BY THE AUTHOR

"If we go somewhere thinking we know everything, we will learn nothing. If we go somewhere, yearning to learn everything, we will learn something."

"I may not know as much as you do, but I know, I know more than you think I do."

"You might not get what you want when YOU want it, but you will get it when HE thinks you need it."

"If we do not rise above the level of our complacency and do something that is bigger than who we are, our purpose in life is diminished. Mediocrity is not on the list."

"Faith is monumental
Knowledge is powerful
Education is vital
Wisdom is priceless."

"Cultures can be interwoven to create a picture, that signifies diversity, inclusion, and acceptance, even when seen through different lenses."

Nekotoryye Studenty

Please tell me what I should do
Some of them don't have a clue
Most of them do use their brain
Some can drive me insane (if I let them)

Some say they just don't have the time
But time is something you can find
Some of them don't have a goal
They tend to think they are too old

I wish they would not think this way
Just live and learn, day by day
Age should never matter
Learning is the main factor

Others think they're not smart
I disagree with all my heart
I believe they can succeed
If they study hard and take heed

2003

STUDENT

Clever, Zealous
Listening, Reading,
Learning
Desiring knowledge to succeed
Exigence
TEACHER
Patient, Passionate
Explaining, Listening,
Imparting
Educator

D.S-R

GOD

Merciful, Powerful
Helping, Giving, Forgiving
Ruler of Life and the Universe

CREATOR

ESL Students' Pledge

I come to English class to learn
Even though my teacher may seem stern
I should always pay attention in class
So when I take my tests I'll pass

I will study hard and do my homework
Because learning another language is no joke
Desire, Determination, and Dedication;
That's the key to complete this class successfully

2006

Pluvo Por Tiel

The strong, steady flow of Mother Nature
descended powerfully on the glistening streets
here. Sharp, piercing, sometimes deafening
sounds cracking intermittently, accompanied
zigzagged movements which invaded the earth's
cover and atmosphere. After what seemed and
sounded like an individualistic rehearsal for an
orchestra, the now constant flow of H2o lingered
as a reminder of Mother Nature's power.

2019

Forte Pluie

Nature's awesome power and beauty were on display last
night in Killeen, Texas, a place not often celebrated for its
weather. Bellowing thunder, fiery lighting, hail and waves
of rain assaulted the night air in concert. At daybreak, calm
returned. Every crevice in the earth was saturated and alive.

Omolumi

Mon Professeur

She sometimes sits on tables, not on chairs
When you're in her class, you're all ears
Her sense of humour can bring on tears
She certainly is someone who cares

Her knowledge of the world is extremely vast
Which gives us a perspective of her intentions
And sometimes she reveals stories from her past.
And they always tie back to International Relations

She surely is someone who deviates from the norm
But is no way objective in any shape or form
Her teaching style is conducive to learning
You can't fall asleep; she keeps the fire burning

Speaking of fire, she likes things hot!
Her affinity for hot sauce to her means a lot
No ketchup and sodium chloride for her
Just bring on the chipotle and the mayo

What did you say? Did I hear the word who?
The French professor who studies jujitsu
We know her-we know who you mean
That's the international queen-Dr. Celine.

2010

D.S-R

Defense of a Nation

Many nations had a vision for 2003
Stop the aggression and conquer the enemy
But who holds the key to this catastrophe
We might not know, but we will see

Foreign nations support American forces
They combined troops together as one
Not disregarding possible losses
Determined by all means to get things done

Top priorities include disarmament and freedom
Parts of the mission to which troops are bound

Now aircraft comb the sky at thousands of feet
Locating targets sans pilots in the seats

Optimism is high, and casualties are low
As troops fight to defeat the elusive foe
When will they return to their homes with glee?
We might know, but we will see.

Kriegssorgen: Mach dir Keine Sorge

Don't worry

About the children
They will be all right
Although when you see them
There'll be a difference in height

Don't worry

About being out of sight
You're in their hearts
Every day-every night

Don't worry

About the bills
They'll get paid
There's a message to be sent And a point to be made

Don't worry

About the grass
It will get cut
It might not be done your way but...........

Don't worry

About the car
It might not look stunning But rest assured
I'll keep it running

D.S-R

About me
I'm grounded and standing tall
I know in my heart God loves us all

When the bombs are all dropped
And the shells are all gone
I know it'll be time

Either way you will come home
And we'll all be waiting
Pourquoi? Parceque c'est la vie

Willkommen Zuruck zu Hause

Many of our warriors are returning home
To families who will no longer be alone
Joy and relief are heartfelt across the nation
As they report to their duty stations riddled with emotion

With wounded bodies, hearts, and souls
Intriguing stories they unfold
Some still face yet another war
Because they know not what's in store

But in this vast and promising land
There will always be someone to lend a hand
Out of the dark hole will emerge a light
And battles will be won where you don't have to fight

Fear is for a Moment, FAITH is Forever

Everyone is at risk, no matter their condition
This "thing", this "thing" favors no particular age, race, gender, or religion
It entered our lives, determined to stay
But solid efforts are being made to eradicate, or keep it at bay

Brutality, homicides, lockdowns and suicides
Civil disobedience resulting in interpersonal and collective violence
In our minds we form these unimaginable, daunting images
Of the historical winter storm that caused loss of lives, school and building closures, and enormous damages

We are witnessing situations
That are crippling the nation
Despite the calamaties that have intruded, (uninvited)
We can focus on some positives that have unfolded

Kindness, closeness, sharing, and caring
Family strengthening and character building
Entrepreneurship, love, religious awareness
All seem to emerge from what seem like an abyss

A Veces en la Vida

Sometimes we have tragedies in our lives
That seem to pierce our hearts like knives
At times we feel we were dealt a bad hand
Finding a solution is like trying to separate sugar
from sand

Wake up daily and pray
Because the One above will lead the way
Have FAITH and do what you need to do
Just know your FAITH will see you throug.

Hurt is cold, pain is bold
Especially when there is no one to hold
It can be excruciating
When you remain waiting for a healing

Which will eventually seep into your life
And put an end to your strife.

C'est la Vie

Sounds of happiness, sounds of sadness
Sometimes bitter-sweet madness
Tears of joy, tears of pain
Again and again and again
No worries, no pressure, no strain

Celebrate the joy, dismiss the pain
We celebrate, we endure
Emotions exist forever more
Others feel the same way too
Yes that's true, not only you

Happiness and sadness sometimes meet
An encounter that is bitter sweet
Happiness will override
The sadness that will subside
In this complex world in which we live

We must find time to stop and give
Give of ourselves with prayers and love
Just as we receive from above.

Vivir Para la Vida

Continue to hope for the best
Situations change with time
Our dreams will manifest
We have no time to whine

Sometimes problems seem to have no reason
So, we keep asking "why"?
But the reason is always on the horizon
Even when everything goes awry

Today might seem dark and meaningless
Darkness will eventually fade away
Life is sometimes tinged with sadness
Tomorrow will be a brighter day

With spurts of love and happiness
Move forward-don't digress.

Explosion of Love, Support, Despite Deadly Act

It did not occur on foreign soil
Nonetheless, the deadly act made your blood boil
A man trained and schooled to lend an ear
Took multiple lives creating an atmosphere of fear

Did he take matters in his hands and act on his own?
As for now, those reasons are unknown
What we do know is the need to mourn the loss
Of the civilians and soldiers of this able-bodied force

Amidst this horrendous tragedy
Emerged an outpouring of love and generosity
In droves they came to show their support
They lined up at hospitals and centers on and off the fort
Tragedies seem to bring people together in unexpected ways

November 5th, 2009, will be remembered for millions of days
Some will still struggle, some will continue to mourn
Despite the severity of this catastrophe, some lessons we
will learn.

Ft. Hood will strive to sustain its pace
And maintain its standing as "The Great Place."

Nov. 6, 2009, 0200

The verdict was read
The sentence was handed down August 28, 2013
Execution
For a man who never denied his action
Victims received Purple Hearts and Defense of Freedom
medals April 10th, 2015.

Warfighter Exercise: Tool for Victory

The success of the mission
Was First Cavalry Division's vision
Stop North Korean aggression
Protect U.S. interest in the region

Top priority was force protection
Throughout the entire division
They conducted offensive operations
While aiding South Koreans

Engineer supported maneuver forces
With guidance from their bosses
They led the way, every day
With insignificant losses

Second brigade; alias "Blackjack"
By no mean any assets lacked
Clearing minefields and new ground
Part of the mission to which they're bound

UAVs combed the sky
At fifteen thousand feet
Located potential targets
Sans pilots in the seats

The Unmanned Aerial Vehicles
Performed reconnaissance missions
Transferred the information
To units in their division

U.S. Air Force provided close air support
Teamed up with 3rd ACR
Who would have thought?

Believe it or not
This unlikely pair
Lessened any fear
And conquered the air

1ST Cav, Division continued its advance
With a show of force that wasn't happenstance
They conquered the objective
They held them at bay
Have you hugged your Cav Patch today?

FAMILIES WATCH 6TH BN. SOLDIERS' BATTLE

It was quiet in Doughboy City Wednesday, except for the infrequent sound of hammering and the delicate crackle of ruddy orange leaves falling from trees. There were no soldiers or tanks in sight. The wind was placid and the sky cloudless. All that was visible, except for the terrain, were the seemingly empty buildings, which produced a ghostly atmosphere.

In the distance, on the rooftop of the Rathaus, soldiers' wives and children waited patiently to witness the battle that was about to take place. **Suddenly**, the sound of bullets ripped through the air and, in a matter of seconds, the area was encircled with a multi-coloured mask of combat smoke.

Fire support then made its way from behind a hill, ran for cover, and began cutting the barbed wire so it could ply through the labyrinthine terrain to seize its target. Almost simultaneously, three armored personnel carriers appeared from behind the hill, rolling ruggedly across the mud-trodden ground, moving towards its target. So far, the attackers were partially successful.

"We managed to seize building "Gulf" and the bottom of building "Bravo," said 2nd Lt. David Hickey, a platoon leader with B Company, 6th Battalion. Now we're attempting to over-run the whole building, but the defenders are putting up a good fight."

The area became crowded, thick with soldiers. As the smoke ascended slowly to the sky, more soldiers advanced swiftly to conquer their objective.

The plan was for the soldiers to work their way to Building "Mike," hitting several other buildings at the same time. B Co. plodded through the slush and mudcaked ground, which resulted from Monday's rain.

In the end-a battle well-fought with many lessons learned.

NBC TRAINING-KEY TO BATTLEFIELD SURVIVAL

In the distance, a soldier drops to the ground. You start to race toward him only to feel your eyes begin to water in a matter of seconds. As you approach him, he is twitching and going into convulsions.

There were no signs of low flying aircraft, no warning sounds from fellow soldiers or from metal on metal.
A bullet did not cause this casualty. This soldier went down on the Nuclear Biologocal and Chemical Battlefield.

The 1972 biological chemical weapons convention prohibits possession of biological weapons, but more nations possess chemical and biological weapons today than at any other time in history.

But, there is hope, because through training, soldiers can survive. The Armed Services continue to conduct Nuclear, Biological and Chemical warfare training.

Soldiers need to train to sustain and improve their ability to survive in a chemical environment. Soldiers from the Brigade Legal Center, McNair Barracks, Berlin, Germany participated in NBC training as part of their regularly scheduled Sergeants' Time.

According to Sgt. 1st Class Jose Perez, Brigade Chemical Non Commissioned Officer in Charge, training and maintenance of the M17A2 protective mask are the two most important aspects of survival during a chemical attack.

"Those factors will keep you alive", he said. Proper donning of the mask is of vital importance. Perez said how you put on your mask will ensure protection, and the first thing soldiers should do after donning it is clear it of any contamination.

Next, seal it by sucking in and then move your head around to make sure the seal is operative.

Perez cited differences between the M17 and masks from other countries, stressing the effectiveness of the M17. He said the eye lenses on the Russians' protective masks are smaller, which limit the vision capability, and some of the masks do not have drinking capabilities.

Including in the training was the proper wear of the protective clothing, following the rule of thumb, which is top over bottom, pants over top of boots. The protective clothing is of high quality and the charcoal liner will protect against all known chemical agents.

"When contamination occurs and the gas starts coming down, it won't seep through any cracks", Perez said.

The use of the M258A1 decontamination kit, which is the training kit for the M58A1 actual kit, was also discussed. The packets for skin contamination are labeled one or two, and the instructions are on the packets.

"You don't want to wait until you're in a contaminated area to begin reading instructions. That's why training is so important", he stressed. Training is highly emphasized and "that's why we always incorporate NBC training with any field training to continue to be combat ready, Perez said.

Private 1st Class Antoine Curry, 5th Bn. Legal Clerk said he did not only learn about the M17.

"I learned a lot. I learned about differences between our technology and for instance the Russians'. The training was beneficial".

Curry said he did not know anything about the M40, so that part of the training was informative and interesting.

The M17, which was introduced in 1959, will be replaced by the M40.

In the 1980s, they began working on a replacement for the M17 protective mask. The XM40 was given the green light for service in 1990 and then named the M40.

According to Lastazar Tucker, Sergeant First Class (Ret), there are some visible differences and improvements in the M40. The mask is equipped with a drinking system that must have appropriate canteen lids or an adapter for other containers.

"This allows the soldier to drink water for long time periods in a chemical environment, he said".

Another aspect of the mask is the external filter canister, which according to Tucker, is much easier to change, compared to the internal cheek filters in the M17. He added that the M40 is also easier to break down.

Because of the improvement in comfort, fit and protection, the M40 protective mask can be worn continuously for eight to twelve hours. Tucker said that the M42A2, Combat Vehicle Crewman Mask is configured the same way as the M40A1with a microphone that is built in for communication.

He noted that the M40 is issued to ground soldiers and comes in small, medium and large. He said, "Soldiers who have masks specially fitted can carry them until their Expiration Term of Service (ETS).

Fast forward to 2009 and the implementation of the M50/51 Joint Service General Purpose Mask (JSGPM).

This mask was designed to protect United States Armed Forces and Allied Forces from Chemical, Biological, Radiologocal and Nuclear (CBRN) threats.

According to James Martin Sr., CBRN Instructor "The M50 mask has dual filters and a new rubber face piece which provides a more comfortable feel and less breathing resistance".

The new suits on the Joint Service Lightweight Integrated Suit Technology (JSLIST) have a liquid repellent coating, provide twenty four hours of protection and can be washed up to six times after training purposes.

According to Martin, "The jackets come with flame resistant hoods to be used with the M51which was designed for crewmen of armored vehicles. Wearing of the hood is determined by the soldiers' Military Occupa tional Speciality (MOS)".

Privates First Class Dainia Sharma and Recha Tillman, students in the CBRN class, said they were learning more than they imagined.

Tillman recalled when she went through the chamber in Basic Training, it was not pleasant for her. "I could actually smell the gas," she said.

On the other hand, Sharma joked, "I had a cold when I went in, and the cold was gone when I came out".

They both agreed that proper training with the mask is extremely important. Sharma said, "Any discoloration of the filters tells you they need to be reserviced".

Tillman added, "You have to change the filters if they are not white".

They remarked that the CBRN classes provide a lot of information necessary for the familiarization and operation of the M50/51.

Some of the design goals for the M50 protective mask were to: Improve performance against chemical and biological agents and nuclear fallout.

Improve field of vision.

Reduce breathing resistance by half over currently fielded masks. Make the mask more comfortable.

Improve equipment compatability e.g JSLIST, optical sites etc. Improve the drinking system for easier use.

2018

POSTVIVADO KARME MORAJ

From Prisoner to First Sergeant

Americans are blessed with many rights The right to possess land, freedom of speech, the right to choose their religion and many more. Imagine for a moment what it would be like to be denied your choice of religion or even worse- to be killed because you made the "wrong" choice. Some people are fortunate to have been born into freedom, but others are not quite as fortunate and have had to live through slavery and war.

At the age of five, war entered his life. He got caught up in a religious battle that made him live in terror for a long time. He witnessed a genocide that took place not in Nazi Germany, but in the state of Croatia, Yugloslavia.

George Zivkovich was born in Zagreb, Yugoslavia. His religion: Serbian Orthodox. To the north of Zagreb is Croatia, a strong clerical land. For anyone not Roman Catholic, life could be difficult.

The Croatians constantly fought to convert the Serbians to Catholicism, putting the Serbians on the defensive for hundreds of years. Zivkovich's first confrontation with the Croatians came one day in 1942 while he was playing outside his house. From that day he would live in concentration camps, labor camps, displaced persons (DP) camps and orphanages for many years.

"I was playing outside alone while my mother was working in the field with some other women," he said. "Our neighbor, Croatian and Ustasi (a name given to those who helped in the extermination of Serbianism and the Orthodox Church) came to our house with a rifle and asked me for my mother. I answered and he told me to take him there.

Zivkovich said he ran ahead of the man yelling to his mother that the Ustasi was behind him. When the other women heard the word "Ustasi", they fled begging his mother to go with them, but she refused to go without her child. Zivkovich and his mother were seized and taken to Jasenovac, one of the many concentration camps located in Croatia.

To Zivkovich, it's one that leaves the most frightening memories of starvation, nightmares and death. "I remember a huge brick wall which separated the women from the men and the boys," said Zivkovich. "Because of my age, I was kept with the women. I remember a little girl being boosted to the top of the wall by some women so that she could see her father, and I still remember the words she screamed as she looked over the wall. "Mama, onu nux bujy, onu nux bujy," which translated means "Mama, they are killing them." The ones who weren't killed died from sickness or starvation.

"Our only meal was a form of corn mush in which they placed nails," he said. According to Zivkvich, children were not spared. They received similar treatment as that of the adults. "Some were sent to special concentration camps which were set up for them, or to labor camps with their mothers, if their mothers were able bodied," he said. "They sent my mother and me to a labor camp in Germany."

Even though this took place over many decades ago, there are instances Zivkovich remembers most vividly. "We were placed in cattle cars to be taken to the labor camp," he said. "On the way there, I remember my mother pointing to the town of Zagreb saying to me "Veedish one zgrade teecece cerogan." (See those buildings, you were born there) "In all my life, even though I knew where I was born, I never admitted it. I always said I was born in Belgrade, because I feared for my life and I detested the catastrophe that took place in the place where I was born," Zivkovitch said.

After several months in the labor camp, they were sent back to a town called Kostanica. There his mother died. "To this day, I don't know how she died. I just remember her laid on a table top where I placed some borrowed candles around her." The years 1942 and 1943 were terrible years for him, because now he was alone with no one to care for him.

One day in 1944, he was captured and questioned by the Ustasi. To escape death, he kept saying that he was Croatian. The next day he was released to get something to eat and he just kept going. He ended up in a restaurant where he saw the man in whose house he once stayed. The man said to him "You're alive! What did you tell them?" "I told them I was Croatian." The man replied "Keep on saying that."

Zivkovich was protected by the Russian Army (allies at the time) who kept hiding him from battalion to battalion so the Ustasi would not find him. Eventually in 1946, they transported him to Ebolie, Italy where he fell under the care of General Zivkovich. George Zivkovich had never revealed his last name for fear of his life, so he was known as George "Malee" (small).

One day, the general asked him how he would like to have the last name Zivkovich and he agreed. From that day he was known as George Zivkovich.

He thought he would be destined to live in DP camps and orphanages for the rest of his life, but the turning point came in 1948 when the general told him about possible adoption.

In 1948, Marko Zivkovich, Wilmerding, Pennsylvania, was reading the American Serbian Daily when the name George Zivkovich caught his eye. Marko read the adoption article and consulted with his wife Martha. This couple had a son whose name was also George Zivkovich. He died at the age of 17. They decided to adopt.

In 1949, George Zivkovich came to the United States. "When I first came to the United States," he said, "it was like coming from hell to heaven. I am grateful to my teachers and friends who accepted me, helped me to overcome my inferior feelings and made me feel worthwhile."

In 1955, Zivkovich received his citizenship. That same day, he joined the U.S. Army to serve almost twenty nine years. He retired as a First Sergeant at the National training Center, (NTC) Fort Irwin, Ca. He said his childhood experiences as a prisoner have made him view the rights and freedom in a different light compared to the average American.

"It makes me appreciate the freedom we have in the United States, and I would do whatever it takes to keep our freedom." "We should never forget the Americans who gave supreme sacrifice for the liberties and freedom we have today," Zivkovich said. "We are not perfect, but compared to other lands we are way ahead of them.

NTC IMPRESSES CSM

He came, he saw, and he was impressed. He was impressed not only with the physical upgrade of the facilities but, above all, with Fort Irwin's leaders and its soldiers.

Command Sergeant Major, (CSM) George L. Horvath 111, command sergeant major, U.S. Forces Command, revisited the National Training Center, (NTC) Fort Irwin.

On a previous visit to the NTC, he participated in rotational unit training, while serving as Command Sergeant Major 111Corps, Fort Hood, TX. As Command Sergeant Major, U.S. Forces Command, his visit to the NTC was twofold.

"The first purpose of my visit was to observe one of our units going through a rotation," said the combat veteran. "Secondly, I wanted to come out here and talk to the soldiers and sergeants at NTC because they are part of U.S. Forces Command. I wanted to let them know how important I think their job is for FORSCOM and the Army. I wanted to get out there and get to know them," said CSM Horvath who joined the Army in his home state of Hawaii in 1960.

"I've seen a lot of physical changes on Ft. Irwin since my last visit. I've seen a tremendous amount of improvement in the quality of the facilities to include the barracks, Welcome Center, Commissary and more. I also saw and heard a lot about changes in the rotational units themselves and their ability to cope with both the environment and the OPFOR (Opposing Forces)."

The NTC's role in preparing FORSCOM's units to fight is of paramount importance, said FORSCOM's top enlisted soldier.

He said he was convinced that the NTC has an immeasurable impact on the Total Army to the point where the Soviets are interested in what is being done at the NTC. "The best trained motorized rifle regiment is stationed right here." "I have been very impressed with the ability of the leaders here at the

NTC, impressed because it takes a level of commitment here at the NTC that is greater than when stationed at other places," he said.

"There is a measure of sacrifice that is larger than is made by other sergeants and other leaders on other posts, because you spend more time in the field and you spend more time away from your families.

You do this repeatedly, and yet each time you do it is with 100 percent commitment to the mission, and you do it well," said the Airborne and Ranger qualified senior non-commissioned officer. CSM Horvath believes that all soldiers are professionals, and as professionals they need to strive for professionalism.

His philosophy for Non Commissioned Officers is that good NCOs must be better than their soldiers. "A good NCO has to be at a bare minimum, at least as good as the soldiers they lead, but what NCOs should strive for is to be better than their soldiers," he said.

"If you're a stripe wearer, you're an NCO and a leader of soldiers, so you have to stay one step ahead of them and stay informed of the latest changes in doctrine as it applies to you, technology and weapon systems. You're the NCO soldiers turn to for their training, and for everything that happens to them," said CSM Horvath.

The command sergeant major fully understands that this is a huge responsibility to be placed on sergeants and because of the vast amount of responsibilities soldiers now have, he feels that NCOs today are much different than they were twenty years ago.

"They can't help but be different. Twenty three years ago when I was a sergeant, my job was relatively easy. I was an infantryman and I had to worry about an Alpha team and a Bravo team. I didn't have any weapon systems except my M1 rifle and an M19A6 30 caliber automatic rifle."

Today, the duties and responsibilities of the NCO are much higher, according to CSM Horvath. Today, that same infantry sergeant, of a Bradley infantry fighting unit, for example, has nine major weapon systems he needs to be smart about. The NCO's responsibility has quadrupled in terms of what he needs to know technologically and tactically.

Additionally, most soldiers are now married and NCOs must also deal with the associated problems young married soldiers' experience. They have to be smart because of the tremendous amount of responsibility that we have placed on these men and women wearing stripes today," he said. "Maybe that's why I'm so proud of them when I think of all the things they have to know to perform professionally." "It's always great to come and see the kinds of soldiers and leaders that I see here. I would love to be a young sergeant in today's Army and be stationed at the NTC".

After 32 years of service CSM Horvath retired from the Army.

NTC Facts: The National Training Center was first established in 1940 as an anti-aircraft gunnery range. In 1942, it was named in honour of Major General George Leroy Irwin, a World War 1 Field Artillery commander. In 1979, it became the Army's National Training Center and since 1981, it has been operated under the US Army Forces Command.

The NTC has been instrumental in preparing Brigade Combat Teams to deploy to a variety of missions, ranging from fighting the Taliban in Afghanistan, preparing reactionary forces on the European continent, assisting with the Ebola crisis in Africa, and fighting the growing threat of ISIS across the Middle East. Today, it is the nation's premiere military training center-Ready and Resilient-leading the Army into the future.

OBSERVER STAFF VISITS 6TH GUARDS MRD, KARLSHORST

For some people Dec. 13 was another routine day. But for a group of military journalists, it was a memorable one. For the first time, the Observer staff, Berlin, Germany, was permitted to visit the Soviet soldiers of the 6th Guards Motorized Rifle Division stationed in Karlshorst, East Berlin.

We went not just as journalists but as soldiers. We went to observe, compare and learn about people who are in the same business we're in-soldiering. The journalists were welcomed by Maj. Karin Streltchenya, who served as an interpreter. He greeted the crew and gave a briefing on how the next three-four hours would be spent. The first stop was at the Soviet museum, which although small, contained much history about the Soviet military, its leaders, historic events and various weapons.

One of the five rooms houses a miniature replica of the Tiergarten Memorial. This war memorial was built to honour the Red Army soldiers who fell in battles during the Second World War. Capt. Andre Stroganof, the museum tour guide said completing the memorial took approximately three months.

The names of about 180 of the soldiers were known. He said Russian journalists were first allowed to visit the memorial during 1988. On one side of this room, a small section was dedicated to Col. Nikoai Erastovich, the first military commander of the former Soviet Sector of Berlin. In another room, huge glass cases with complete military uniforms from various forces lined the walls.

After a seemingly lengthy tour of the museum, we were escorted to another room and introduced to Lt. Col. Taranov Alexander, the deputy brigade commander. His time in the military belies his youthful appearance. Alexander, 34, a 17-year veteran of the Soviet military, had been serving in Berlin for three months. He was quiet and reserved and, somewhat like an obedient child, spoke only when spoken to. But when he spoke, his voice was strong, commanding and authoritative.

Alexander said the Soviet Army recruits soldiers in the Soviet Union. Within three-five days, they are sent to Berlin to undergo basic training for a month. He said the Soviet Army recruits soldiers twice annually, replacing 25 percent during the Spring and 25 percent during December. The division has about 2,000 soldiers including officers, with a female officer in a signal unit.

Unlike American soldiers, he said married officers serve five years, single soldiers serve three, and they have an annual vacation. American soldiers are allowed thirty days of leave, which they can take at different times during the year.
We also went to the dining facility, which was quite bare, because lunch time was over.

When the commander was asked if soldiers being overweight in the Army posed a problem, he said, "Eta ne vajknee" (It's not important). He said as long as the soldiers could do their jobs and complete the mission, being overweight was not a major factor.

I had an opportunity to practice some Russian, and we all left the installation with a broader perspective of those soldiers, their insight and the unit.

THIRD WORLD HEATS UP BERLIN

The weather was pretty hot outside, but not nearly as hot as the inside of the Tempodrom where Third World performed. The heat came not from the sun but from the fiery sounds of the band.

The group opened the show with its sound "Ninety six Degrees in the Shade," and at the sound of the first note, the crowd was on its feet moving bodies rhythmically to the penetrating pulsating beat. "I think the show was really good," said Sgt. Michael Brown, H&S Company, Field Station, Berlin.

Brown who is pretty familiar with the group's music originally saw them perform in Greece. "They always put on a great performance, he said. The people who did not show up missed a good concert."

Civilian employee, Felicia Dove shared the same feelings as Brown. "It was an excellent performance, she said. "Their music enticed my entire body. They displayed a variety of Reggae music. I especially liked the concerto piece they played. It reminded me of some type of Reggae symphony."

Third World, founded in 1973 in Kingston, Jamaica by keyboarder Michael "Ibo" Cooper and guitarist Stephen "Cat" Coore, is one of the world's best known Reggae bands. It's not very difficult to put a finger on the reason for the group's success.

They exude a powerful, defined distinctive sound-a sound that propelled them to stardom in 1978 with their first worldwide hit "Now that we found love." Ever since that release, the band has its "Spot of Honor" in the Reggae Music Hall of Fame. The group members all were born in Jamaica and have been performing together for decades.

What keeps them together and inspires them to sing the songs they sing? Similar views and vibrations. "We live in a very inspiring part of the world, Ibo said. Someone feels inspired, gets fired up and writes a song."

Inspiration comes in many forms. Caribbean sunshine, creative sounds, blue skies and beautiful people are some of the factors that create the inspiration when writing songs.

"An economic or even a political situation can also be an inspiring force," said "Rugs" the lead vocalist. He stressed the band's joy at being able to perform in Berlin during changed times. "I'm glad the walls are down and the borders are free, he said. People need to be free so they can be who they want to be."

CAVALRY CSM SELECTED FOR 1ST AD TOP NCO SLOT

Like the other candidates' packets his packet was impressive, but he was even more impressive in person Oct. 25 in Bad Kreuznach, Germany. Command Sgt. Maj. Kenneth O. Preston, 3rd Brigade, was selected from a field of sergeants major for the 1st Armored Division, U.S Army Europe and Seventh Army.

According to Preston, the 1st Armored Division's current sergeant major is scheduled to report to 3rd Army Dec. 20. "This created a vacancy which opened up a slate to sergeants major who have served in a brigade position for one year or more." He submitted his packet which consisted of a biography, photo copy of 2-1 and 2a, and letters of recommendation from the brigade and division commanders.

He said all packets were sent to the Department of the Army, DA, where various sergeants major including the Sergeant Major of the Army reviewed them. After background checks were conducted, the packets were forwarded to the commanding general, Maj. Gen. George Casey, who then set up interviews with the nominative sergeants major.

Preston's interview was conducted Oct. 25, and on Oct. 28 he received a phone call informing him of his selection. "I am truly honored to be selected for this position," said Preston. He said he was especially honored to have been selected because of the caliber of the sergeants major who vied for the position.

"I knew several of the sergeants major who were considered, and I can tell you they are the cream of the Sergeant Major crop," he said."

His wife Karen echoes similar sentiments about Preston. "He works extremely hard, and I think he's the best man for the job, she said. I know he will do a wonderful job. He'll be good at it, and I'll be behind him no matter what." They have three children, Valerie, 24, Kenny 22, and Michael 18. Preston presents a silent positive image that seems to confirm his potential for accomplishment.

"This new position will carry a different level of responsibility for me. Decisions will be made at division level and will have an impact on a significantly larger number of soldiers, but I am ready to shoulder the responsibility.

Command Sgt. Maj. Paul Inman, 1st Cavalry Division Sergeant Major, said he was extremely proud that Preston got the position. He said he was very deserving of the position, and it was also great news for the 1st cavalry Division.

Preston, who is scheduled to report to his new assignment in December, said he will definitely miss the 1st Cav. "I started my career in the Army as a private right here in Headquarters Company, 2-8th Cav in November, 1975, where I served as a loader, driver and gunner on the battalion commander's tank," he said.

He left for Germany in February, 1978 as a sergeant and returned in September 1996 as a sergeant major. He graduated from the Sergeant Major's Academy in the summer of 1996 and joined 3-8 Cav. in September when the battalion was deploying to Kuwait.

Preston said that during his career, he has had two very rewarding tours in Germany. The first tour was as a tank commander and company master gunner in Gelnhausen and the second tour was as a first sergeant, A Troop, 11th ACR.

He seems to have no doubt that this third tour will be equally, if not more promising and fulfilling as the previous ones.

After nearly thirty six years of service, Sergeant Major of the Army, Kenneth O. Preston, retired March 1, 2011 as the longest serving SMA.

EINMAL GETRENNT, JETZ WIEDERVEREINT

More than six decades ago, the fear of the unknown entered the lives of millions, and lives were instantly altered. When the Berlin Wall was erected, it instantly showed the separation of two cities. The Soviets claimed East Berlin and allies controlled the West. After a while citizens "on both sides of the fence", still fearful, began to accept the reality of the situation.

Twenty nine years ago, that fear was replaced by hope and happiness. On November 9th, 1989, a massive influx of people ignited a state of euphoria when they advanced through the most famous crossing point on Friedrichstrasse.

It was one of the most historic moments of all time, and the city of Berlin was transformed. This historic move certainly captured the attention of millions of people free and not free. They came on foot, some by bicycles, and of course others by the notoriously popular Trabant.

East Berlin always seemed to have a dark overcast, but to me, that darkness disappeared and was replaced with light and hope on November ninth. I remember that day quite vividly.

> Supervisor: Is your television on?
> Me: No. Why?
> Supervisor: Turn it on. You need to get to the office
> ASAP.
> Me: Okay.

NEWS FLASH: Chaos at Checkpoint Charlie, which was opened ten days after East Berlin, was sealed off. There was chaos at other checkpoints also, but Checkpoint Charlie, being the most famous point through the Berlin Wall, bore the brunt of the excitement. "Checkpoint C" had been in operation since

August 1961, ten days after the wall was built. When the wall came down, the gateway to freedom opened permanently June 22nd 1990 and Checkpoint Charlie was removed.

In May 1989, Hungary decided to tear down its border fence, with Austria opening a first hole in the iron curtain. That action in some way represented the first cracks in the wall. Although the Berlin Wall stood, more than 13,000 East Germans crossed into Hungary on "vacation" and defected to the West. Three million East Germans escaped between 1945 and 1961.

On November ninth, the border between East and West Germany would be opened for private trips abroad. Thousands of people proceeded to the border to get to the West. They began to chip away at the wall, using anything that would afford them an opportunity to not only destroy the wall, but to retain a piece of history.

The topographical view from a helicopter was a sight to behold, and as equally exciting as being in the midst of the mayhem. There was a time, before the collapse of the wall, when security, upon entering EastBerlin was so uniformed, rigid and coordinated. Soldiers had to travel in uniform.

I remember sitting on the bus at Checkpoint Charlie and being given instructions: "Look straight ahead. Do not look to the right or the left. Keep your palms down on your thighs." Meanwhile a couple of the border guards were "inspecting" the bus internally and externally. A combination of emotions gushed through my body. I was nervous, excited and curious.

Now, the border guards, having no instructions on how to handle the situation, basically surrendered to the people. Some guards were not opposed to taking the few steps, literally, to the promise land when no one was looking.

I think the day the Berlin Wall fell, new lives were created. Imagine what they were going through, being part of the city, but separated by a man-made structure that would prohibit or limit interaction with families and friends.

There are a few famous phrases associated with Berlin

and its state: Most of us are familiar with "Wir sind ein Volk". I remember speaking with some of the refugees and trying to imagine their emotions. From the East, many people were not privy to the modernization and the expansion of West Berlin. There, they were all part of the same city but divided by a wall. They were strangers in their own land.

Something gripped my soul when I looked into the eyes of both the young and the elderly. They were experiencing freedom. The West Berliners set up numerous soup kitchens and temporary lodging areas throughout the city.

The city provided cots, beds and food for thousands, because many of them just crossed the checkpoint without family or a place to stay. They also received "Kostenloses Geld" as a gift to assist them in the beginning of their new journey.

Two phrases were especially common on that day; "Danke Schon" and "Bitte Schon". These phrases continuously echoed throughout the crowds.

Familiarity surfaces with these two four-word quotations- "Ich bin ein Berliner" and "Tear down this wall". The latter is exactly what transpired on November 9th.

The end of the Cold War left the west, including the U.S, with no definite paradigm as to where, when and how force should be used. Checkpoint Charlie was on the front of the struggle between East and West Berlin.

U.S military policemen, British Royal Military Police and French Gendarmes served at the Checkpoint for multiple decades amidst times of détente, periods of high tension and questionable moments. They should be recognized and remembered for their commitment.

On December 31st, 1989, Berliners had the wildest party ever. While the wall was crumbling, thousands of Berliners were singing "I've been looking for freedom", in ENGLISH.

When the wall came down, the gateway to freedom opened permanently, and on June 22nd 1990, Checkpoint Charlie was permanently removed.

On November ninth, the foundation was unable to withstand the breakthrough of freedom.

Bitte Schon

You are welcome

Danke Schon
Thank you

Kostenloses Geld
Free money

Ich bin ein Berliner
I am a Berliner

Wir sind ein Volk
We are one Nation

Einmal Getrennt
Once Divided

Jetzt Vereint
Now United

Dear Teacher,

Today we have to say goodbye to you teacher and the classmates, much to our regret. Frank and I will take another direction out of Texas. We don't want to say goodbye without expressing our feelings about you.

You are an excellent teacher, very good and with a degree of incredible tolerance, to tolerate us as students. As a person you are an incredible humanitarian, full of affection and a good heart. Thanks teacher, we don't have words to thank you enough for what we have learned.

Thanks for everything you did for me and my son. God bless you and give you good health, so you can continue teaching with dedication and devotion as done.

Cordially Yours
Lourdes and Frank Hernandez

C'est avec un grand plaisir que j'ai decide de participer a ce projet. J'avais pris l' anglais comme une seconde language avec la meilleure ESL instutitrice durant le printemps a l'automne deux mille neuf. Mon experience etait riche.

Quand je venais juste des Etats-Unis, je ne pouvasi ni communiquer encore moins comprendre ce que les autres disaient. J'etais tres timide de communiquer avec une langue etrangere que je ne maitriser pas.

C'est alors que j'avais pris la decision d'approfondir ma connaissance sur la langue anglaise. Mes camarade de classe et moi avions appris beaucoup de choses comme a con- juguer les temps au present, passe, futur et present progres- sive. Nous avions aussi fait beacoup de grammaire, tel que l'utilisation du ponctuation, de l'article, preposition en an- glais.

La lecture etait aussi importante parce que ca nous permettrait de prononcer les mots corrrectement, d'eleminer notre accent et en meme temps, notre vocabulaire devenait de plus en plus riche. Pour chaque lecture, y'avait de nouveaux mots a apprendre et pour chaque nouveau mot appris, l'eleve devrait ecrire une sentence.

Mon activite prefere etait l'information hebdomadaire. Chaque matin, on devrait amener une information que nous devrions partager avec le reste de la classe. Cela nous permettrait d'etre informer et de comprendre ce qui se passé aux Etats-Unis et le reste du monde.

Il y'avait aussi les petites sorties que l'institutrice organisait. Un des plus symboliques etait notre visite chez le maire de Killeen Timothy Hancock avec qui j'ai eu l'occasion de questioner sur l'immigration.

Mes camarades de classe etaient une seconde fa- mille pour moi. Elles me manquent tous, Seoyoung, Zhenya et Kim. Elles etaient vraiment tres gentilles et supportives. Bien que je n'ai passé que sept mois la-bas, mon institutrice m'appelle ou m'envoie de l'email pour s'acquerir de mes nouvelles et voire comment je pro- gresse avec mes classes.

Elle veut vraiment que ses eleves reussissent. Je suis tres fortune de l'avoir comme institutrice parce que après un certains moment, je pouvais ecrire et m'expri- mer en anglais. Je suis plus confiante a moi meme et maintenant je suis au college pour devenir operationelle.

Sokhna Daga Fall,
Senegal, Africa

It's an immense pleasure for me to participate in this activity. I took English as a Second Language with the best

English teacher ever during the Spring-Fall of 2009. My experience was very great.

Taking an ESL class really shaped my knowledge of academic English. When I first came in the United States I could not communicate at all with other people or understand them. I was too shy to talk in a foreign language and I also used to pronounce the English words very badly.

Then I took this class. There, I learned a lot. My classmates and I studied a lot of grammar such as the use of correct punctuation, articles, prepositions... We also learned how to use the English tenses by doing a lot of conjugations such as the present tense, present progressive, and past perfect. Look at the key word as a guide... Reading was very important because it helped me articulate the English words correctly, get rid of my accent a little and at the same time, my vocabulary was getting richer.

After each lecture, we used to write some sentences about each new word we learned. My favorite part was the news. The students were supposed to write and bring news articles and read them in front of the class. We got a lot of important information that helped us understand what was going on around the world and debate it.

Without forgetting the field trips, I am still saving my coins that I received from the mayor of Killeen. Anyway, it was really a great experience. My classmates used to be a second family for me.

I miss them all, Seoyoung, Zhenya, Kim... my instructor who is so nice and supportive even though I had been there for like seven months.

She will call or send an email to check on me, ask how I am doing with my classes. She really wants her students to succeed. I am just very lucky to have had her as my instructor because, not only could I write and express myself, but I was also able to enroll in other college courses in order to realize my career aspirations.

Sokhna Daga Fall
Senegal, Africa

On July 29, I got a text message from my husband. The text was, "You can go to ESL class tomorrow". I had been waiting for a few years years.

On the first day of class, I was excited and afraid. I couldn't concentrate because I was too nervous.

My teacher always wants us to raise our hands when we want to talk.

But that was really hard for me, because I thought

"what if I say something incorrectly? What if I'm wrong? What if she thinks my questions are weird?"

Also, what if my classmates sneer at me?" All these thoughts made me afraid.

After one week. She told us something. It was very touching and gave me motivation.

She said, don't be afraid to ask. If someone corrects you, say thank you." This is how you learn English. Also, she doesn't say "No". Instead she says "someone else, or nice try." If you are wrong, it's ok. Don't be afraid to ask. If someone corrects you, say thank you. This is how you learn English." This challenged me to think when I gave a wrong answer.

I think, when I was a teenager, I didn't always ask questions and wasn't always interested. I was a normal student. But here in this class, I always try to find the answers, ask lots of questions and study at home. This is something I learned from this class.

Failure is not the end; it will take me to success. I will keep trying and I won't forget this class. I really appreciate my teacher "Ms.Google." This is something I learned from the class. My teacher gives me a reason to learn and challenges me.

Jin Ha Verheyen
Korea

7월 29일 나는 남편으로부터 문자메세지를 받았다. 그 문자는 내일부터 내가 ESL 수업에 갈 수 있다는 내용이었다. 나는 그것을 8년 동안 기다려왔었다.

첫 수업 날 나는 두렵고 흥분되었다. 너무 불안해서 집중하기도 힘들었다.
나의 선생님은 우리가 할 말이 있다면 항상 손을 들고 말하면 된다고 말씀하셨다.
그러나 나는 그것이 힘들었다. '내 문법이 틀렸으면 어떡하지?, 질문이 무엇인가 잘못 되었다면? 선생님께서 내 질문이 이상하다고 생각하시지는 않을까?, 같은반 친구들이 나를 비웃지는 않을까? ' 이런 생각들이 나를 두렵게 만들었기 때문이다.

일주일이 지난 후, 선생님께서 우리에게 말씀하셨다.
"네가 틀려도 괜찮아. 질문하는 것을 두려워 하지마. 만약 다른 사람이 너의 문법을 고쳐준다면 고맙다고 말하면 돼. 그게 영어를 배울 수 있는 방법이야."
그 말은 내가 무엇인가 틀렸을 때에도 나를 도전 할 수 있게 만들었다.

내가 십 대였을 때, 나는 질문도 잘 하지 않았고 그런 것들에 흥미도 없었다.
하지만 이 수업을 통해서 항상 답을 찾기 위해 질문하고 노력하며 공부해야 한다는 것을 배웠다.

선생님께서는 내가 공부를 해야 하는 이유를 느끼게 해 주셨고 도전하게 만드셨다.
실패는 끝이 아니라 그것이 너를 성공으로 데려가 줄 것이라 말씀하셨다.
나는 계속 노력할 것이며 이 수업을 잊지 않을 것이다. 나는 내 선생님 "미세스 구글"께 매우 감사드린다.

진하Verheyen
한국

ESL is an unbelievable help for me. I felt lost after my arrival in the USA. I had no knowledge of English and I knew no one. I tried to teach myself but was unsuccessful. A radical change happened after I started ESL.

My abilities with the English language improved drastically, for which I have the competent and extremely patient teacher to thank. In her personification, I found what I was looking for in a teacher; someone who is very demanding of her students, but at the same time offers an excellent classroom environment.

In class, I received answers to all my questions, and they were not few. They cover not only English grammar and pronunciation, but normal items from everyday life. Every immigrant knows what I am saying.

An added benefit I have received from ESL is the many people from different countries and cultures I have met. I have established a lot of friendships that mean a lot to me. I recommend that all immigrants who want to make America their home attend ESL classes.

Izabela Quinn
Czech Republic

ESL je pre mna neopisatelna pomoc.

Po mojom prichode do USA som sa citila byt stratena. Neovladala som tunajsi jazyk a nepoznala som tu niko- ho. Snazila som sa ucit anglictinu ako samouk, ale be- zuspesne.
Radikalny obrat nastal ked som zacala chodit do ESL. Moje jazykove znalosti sa podstatne zlepsili vdaka mojej kompetentnej a neuveritelne trpezlivej ucitelke. V jej osobe som nasla presne to co som hladala. Niekoho kto je narocny na studentov, ale zaroven im poskytuje vzorovu vyucbu.
V skole dostavam odpoved na vsetky moje otazky – a tych nie je malo. Netykaju sa iba gramatiky a vyslov- nosti, ale aj normalneho bezneho zivota. Kazdy pri- vandrovalec vie o com pisem.
Co ma pre mna nezaplatitelnu hodnotu je to, ze v ESl som spoznala mnoho ludi z roznych krajin sveta. Nadviazala som tu priatelstva ktore mi znamenaju velmi vela.
Odporucam kazdemu cudzincovi ktory sa chce udomacnit v Amerike, studovat v ESL.

Izabela Quinn
Czech Republic

In 2010, I decided to move to The United States and make Texas my permanent home. Once here, I immediately started my search for a job. Due to my limited English skills, it was hard to find the kinds of jobs I was looking for.

After six months of unsuccessful attempts, I decided to try working as a Substitute Teacher. Due to my college degree, I was able to teach, but only felt comfortable with Spanish classes. That is when I heard about the Adult Education Program and how they help English learners.

In summer 2011, I was enrolled to take English class with whom I consider the best instructor ever. I took sixty hours of intense English. She was a great instrument through my journey to learning. She gave me lots of learning tools, motivated me to read more, learn new words, write essays, and make presentations which I did every day.

In the end, I think part of a student's success comes from within (self-motivation), but you always need the right person (instructor) to guide you and keep you on track. She also gave me the confidence to believe in myself and believe that I could get the right job. Thank you for being the instrument, for motivating, believing, and inspiring me.

After completing sixty hours in ESL with her I became part of the KISD family for seven years. Presently, I am an ESL Instructor with the Adult Education Program in CTC. Nine years ago, I would have never dreamt of becoming an English Instructor. That is why, every time I get in front of my class, I try to give them hope, to be a good inspiration and to motivate them just as my instructor did for me.

Learning a new language, especially after your forties, is not an easy goal; but if you persevere, work hard and practice, you can achieve it. I'm still learning every day, and that's what I tell my students. Do not give up; it is never too late to learn!

Elizabethh Burgos-Alvarez

En el 2010, decidí mudarme a los Estados Unidos y hacer de Texas mi hogar permanente. Una vez aquí, comencé mi búsqueda para encontrar un trabajo. Debido a mis limitadas habilidades en el idioma inglés, me fue difícil encontrar el tipo de trabajo que estaba buscando.

Después de seis meses de intentos fallidos, decidí trabajar como maestra sustituta. Debido a mi título universitario, pude enseñar, pero sólo me sentía cómoda con las clases de español. Durante este tiempo, escuché sobre el Programa de Educación para Adultos y cómo este programa ayuda a aprender inglés.

En el verano de 2011, me inscribí para tomar la clase de inglés con quien considero la mejor instructora que he conocido. Tomé sesenta horas de inglés intensivo. La instructora fue un gran instrumento a través de mi travesía al conocimiento. Ella me mostró muchas herramientas para aprender inglés, me motivó a leer más, aprender nuevas palabras, redactar ensayos y dar presentaciones lo que hice diariamente.

Finalmente, creo que parte del éxito del estudiante viene de adentro (automotivación), pero uno siempre necesita a la persona correcta (instructor) para guiarte y mantenerte en el camino correcto. Ella también me dio la confianza para creer en mí misma y creer que yo podía conseguir el trabajo que quería. Gracias por ser el instrumento, por motivarme, inspirarme y creer en mí.

Después de completar sesenta horas en el curso de inglés como segundo idioma (*English as a Second Language)* con la instructora, me integré a la familia del Distrito Escolar Independiente de Killeen (*Killeen Independent School District)* durante siete años. Al presente, soy Instructora de ESL con el Programa de Educación para Adultos en Central Texas College. Nueve años atrás, jamás hubiera soñado en convertirme en instructora de inglés. Por tal motivo, cada vez que me presento frente a mi aula, intento dar esperanza a mis alumnos, ser una buena inspiración y motivarlos de igual manera que mi instructora lo hizo por mí.

Aprender un nuevo idioma, especialmente después de los cuarenta, no es una meta fácil; pero si perseveras, trabajas duro y practicas lo aprendido, lo puedes lograr. Yo continúo aprendiendo todos los días, y eso les digo a mis alumnos. ¡No te rindas, nunca es demasiado tarde para aprender!

Elizabeth BurgosAlvarez

When I registered for the English as a Second language course at Central Texas College, I already had some knowledge of English that I had learned on my own. I had taken some classes in Middle School, and I wish I had paid more attention. I still was not able to carry on a conversation.

I usually read, watch movies in English and listen to the people around me in the United States.

When I started taking ESL classes at CTC, on the Ft. Hood Campus, I began to work on my pronunciation and to form sentences on my own, along with daily exercises assigned to me. I began to put into practice what I was learning, when I had conversations with people who spoke only English.

Sometimes, we have to make sacrifices, and if we are not willing to do it, it will be more difficult for us to learn English. For example, watching movies in English, when you are used to watching them in your native language, is a sacrifice worthwhile, even though you can't understand and enjoy the movie as you would like.

I had to discontinue my classes because of military duties, but I am leaving with a firmer understanding of English, and I have progressed to the Advanced level in the Best Plus Area of the course. Hopefully, the knowledge I obtained and will continue to obtain will be permanent.

Personally, the ESL course at CTC made me expand my mind in a definite way of learning English grammar. I am much more confident with myself since I know that I am not alone on this ship. Now I am able to speak English and participate in conversations without hesitating. I learned to have confidence in myself, and I think that has a great part in learning.

Abdiel M. Martinez
Puerto Rico

Cuando me inscribí para el curso de inglés como segundo idioma en Central Texas College, ya tenía algunos conocimientos de inglés que había aprendido por mi cuenta. Había tomado algunas clases en la escuela secundaria y desearía haber prestado más atención. Todavía no podía mantener una conversación.

Usualmente leo, veo películas en inglés y escucho a las personas que me rodean en los Estados Unidos.

Cuando comencé a tomar clases de ESL en CTC, en el Ft. Hood Campus, comencé a trabajar en mi pronunciación y a formar oraciones por mi cuenta, junto con los ejercicios diarios que me asignaron. Comencé a poner en práctica lo que estaba aprendiendo, cuando tuve conversaciones con personas que solo hablaban inglés.

A veces, tenemos que hacer sacrificios, y si no estamos dis-puestos a hacerlo, será más difícil para nosotros aprender inglés.

Por ejemplo, mirar películas en inglés, cuando estás acostumbrado a verlas en tu idioma nativo, es un sacrificio que vale la pena, aunque no puedas entender y disfrutar la película como te gustaría.

Tuve que suspender mis clases debido a los deberes militares, pero me voy con una comprensión más firme del inglés, y he progresado al nivel avanzado en el área Best Plus del curso. Con suerte, el conocimiento que obtuve y continuaré obteniendo será permanente.

Personalmente, el curso de ESL en CTC me hizo expandir mi mente en una forma definitiva de aprender gramática inglesa.

Tengo mucha más confianza en mí mismo porque sé que no estoy solo en este barco. Ahora puedo hablar inglés y participar en conversaciones sin dudarlo. Aprendí a tener confianza en mí mismo, y creo que eso tiene una gran parte en el aprendizaje.

Abdiel M. Martínez
Puerto Rico

I am not a good author or speaker, but I just want to say how the ESL class has helped me, and talk about my first experience in the United States.

I took an English class, and I was a swimming coach in my country. When I came to the United States, I started my English as a Second language class on the Fort Hood campus, in 2015. At that time, I didn't speak and understand English. Everything here was completely different.

I learned a lot of information about the American culture, food and language. I learned how to help each other in difficult times. The first day I was so shy and afraid. I didn't know my teacher and classmates. Everything was new for me. All my classmates were from different countries and spoke different languages. When they talked to me, I just smiled, was afraid and worried.

After the introductions, I felt comfortable when I saw my kind, nice teacher and classmates every day. I was happier and tried to learn more English. I loved her teaching method and she pushed us to study more and learn English. We learned a lot of grammar and vocabulary. One of the important things I learned was grammar.

Every day, we had to bring a new word with the definition, and at the end of the class the teacher would ask each one of us, for example, "Nadia, what's your word"? If we remembered it, we would have to say it with the correct pronunciation. Every day I learned a new word, and that increased my vocabulary. I always liked when we did the ten spelling word exercise.

Another interesting part of the class for me was when we prepared and shared food from our countries. We had to write a recipe and describe it, in front of the class, in English. That was one of the best ways to practice our speaking and to learn about each other's country and culture.

I received a certificate at the end of the course. During the ESL class, I found the best teacher and the best friends.

I had fun speaking and understanding English. I still have a relationship with my teacher and my classmates. The best memory I still have from my class is, if you didn't know or didn't understand something, nobody laughed at you even if their level was higher. I am so lucky to have that experience. Now I have a job, and I still study on the CTC Main Campus.

Nadia Hosseinzadeh
Iran

اسم من نادیا حسین زاده. من اهل ایران هستم من نویسنده و سخنران خوبی نیستم اما فقط میخواهم توضیح بدم چگونه ایی اس ال کلاس به من کمک کرد و اولین تجربه ی من چه چیزی بود من ایی اس ال کلاس را در سال 2015 شروع کردم در ان مدت من نه میتوانستم انگلیسی صحبت کنم یا اینکه متوجه بشم من در ایران کلاسهای انگلیسی را گذرانده بودم و در رشته ی حقوق لیسانس گرفتم و در مراحل باز کردن دفتر ثبت اسناد رسمی بودم و همچنین در رشته ی شنا مربیگری میکردم اما همه چیز در امریکا متفاوت بود چیزهای خیلی زیادی در مورد فرهنگ و غذا وزبان امریکا یاد گرفتم چگونه یاد گرفتم در شرایط سخت به همدیگر کمک کنیم روز اول من خیلی خجالتی و ترسیده بودم معلم و همکلاسیهایم را نمیشناختم همه چیز برایم تازه بود همه ی همکلاسیهایم از کشورهای مختلف بودند با زبانهای مختلف زمانی که انها با من حرف میزدنت من فقط لبخند میزدم و عرق میریختم و ترس و نگرانی در وجودم بالا میگرفت بعد از معرفی هر کدام از همکلاسیها کمی احساس ارامش و راحتی کردم وقتی همکلاسیها و و معلم خوب و مهربان را دیدم هر روز خوشحالتر میشدم و تلاش بیشتری برای یادگیری داشتم روش تدریس معلم را خیلی دوست داشتم و همیشه مارو تشویق میکرد خواندن و یادگیری انگلیسی بیشتر در این کلاسها مهمترین چیزی که یاد گرفتم گرامر و کلمات جدید انگلیسی بود زیرا هر روز باید به دیکشنیری نگاه میکردیم و یک کلمه ی جدید با معنی کلمه به انگلیسی را مینوشتیم و یاد میگرفتیم و همچنین هر روز باید 10 کلمه دیکته داشتیم و من خلی این را دوست داشتم چون برای یادگیری املا خیلی کمک میکرد بخش خوب و سرگرم کننده ی کلاس جشنهایی بود که در ان غذا و فرهنک کشورهای مختلف به نمایش گذاشته میشد من توانستم که در اخر دوره مدرک بگیرم و عکس بگیریم و غذا بخوریم در طول کلاسهای ایی اس ال توانستم بهترین معلم و دوستهای خوب پیدا کنم خیلی به من خوس گذشت در طول دوره و توانستم انگلیسی یاد بگیرم و صحبت کنم هنوز با معلم وهمکلاسیهایم رابطه دارم و الان بهترین ونزدیکترین افراد در زندگی من انها هستند بهترین خاطره ای که از ای اس ال کلاس دارم این است که اگر شما نمتوانستید حرف بزنید یا متوجه بشید هیچ کس شما را مسخره نمیکند بلکه تلاش میکند به شما کمک کند و با صبر و حوصله با شما کار میکند من خیلی خوش شانس بودم که توانستم با انها اشنا شوم الان من در جایی مصغول به کار هستم و هنوز در سی تی سی مشغول یاد گرفتن هر چه بیشتر انگلیسی هستم و برای وارد شدن به کلاسهای دانشگاهی تلاش میکنم.

Nadia Hosseinzadeh
Iran

جامانربلا اذه ؛ اهريياغبن ييقطقنلل.ةيناث ةغلك ـ ةيزيلجنإلا ةغللا
ثدحت تا ريوطت يف ىلع بالطلا نودعاسي نيذلا نيملعملا اهيدل
،ةغللاو ،ةباتكلاو ،ةءارقلاو مهاراهمو مهفلا يف ةيزيلجنإلا ةغللا
ةغللاو ةدعاسمو بالطلا ىلع أن اوحبصي رثكأ ةقالط يف ةيزيلجنإلا.
سانلا عم لصاوتلل ةقم ىلإ لوألا تئيج امدنع دنع عرفأ أن ان نكل مل حارف ةغللا
يف مجرتملا لك ةجاجح تنك تنك دنع دعوم عم بالطلاب. اصوصخو
تقو. ثم أدركت ينينأ ةجاجح ةذالذلل ىلإ باهذلا ،يلثم صخش وأ انأ ال
لصحلا ال ينينأ ةيناث كلغك ةيزيلجنإلا ةغللا ميلعتل عفدا عم لك أملأ
ام يفكي نم لاملا. تمقو ثحبب نع سورد ةيناجم ،ةكنكو تكرابم
يفوت ليل أن أ يل يتأ ام ىلإ روثعلا ىلع هذه فص يسردملا اناجملا ىلع مغرلا نم قرقرغتسا نم
ةيعفادلاو سامحلا نم اريبك اردق عم تئيج ةسردملاا.

من قاشلل لمعلا ردقو ريثكلا فصلاب تعمتمتا أن انآلا يقودصق
امدنع ةحيحص صصح لمج مادختسا ةيفيك تملعت أتعلم ةسردملا. دقل ةجاح ماهردملاا. دقل
يف يلخدلل موي لوأ لاعفألا يف يأ مادختسا ةيفيك تملعت أتكلم.
كلذب ابجعأ انآلاو ، لبق نم حيحص وحنلا نحن أن أن نكل مل فصلا.

وفي هذه فصلا تيبحأ ةتوافتم ةيقرع ةيفلخلاو ةيفاقثلا
ةغللا جامانربلا هذه نا يأر يف. و ملاعلا ءاحنأ فلتخم نم عيمجلل
تاياضيرلل ملعتو مهفلا ىلع دعاسي ةيناث ةغلك ةيزيلجنالا
ةغللاو نومهفي ال نيذلا بالطلا. نكمي ةقيرطلا لهسأ يف ريخاتلاو
لثم تاقبطلا تامولعملاو. ألأحيانا تاعلعم وأ ةءارق، ألأ ةيزيلجنإلا ال مهنكمي مهف
تارايخ خيرات تايالولا ةدحتملا نوكت نعصب ريثكا مهفل اذإ اونوكا ال
ةيزيلجنإلا ةغلل ةطيسبلا دعاوق نوفرعي.

رم هنأ امك ةيزيلجنإلا ةغللا مهفو نيسحتل ىلع علطتأ أن ألبقتسم مستقبلأ
ةغللا يه ةيزيلجنإلا ةغللا نال ،مويلا ملاع يف حاجنلا قيقحتل يويح يوويح
يلودلا.
مل سال دادو : فرط نم

ايقيرفأ – نادوسلا بونج ةيروهمج

ESL stands for English as a Second Language.

This ESL program has teachers who help students to develop their speaking, writing, reading, and com- prehension skills with the English language and help students become more fluent in English.

When I first came to the United Sates I didn't know English. I had difficulty communicating with people, especially when I had a doctor's appoint- ment. I needed to have an interpreter with me all the time. Then I realized that I need to go to school.

For someone like me, I can't afford to pay for ESL classes because I don't make enough money. I searched for free classes; I was blessed to find this class for free even though it took me a long time on the waiting list.

When they called me to come to class I came with a great deal of enthusiasm and motivation. Believe me, now I am enjoying the ESL class.

I appreciate the hard work that I get from our class. I learned how to use correct sentences when I speak. I learned how to use verbs my first day in class. I didn't know the correct grammar, and now I am so im- pressed.

I like the varying ethnic and cultural back- grounds of everyone in the class. In my opinion, ESL programs help me break down and learn mathematics and History in a way that is easier for me because I have English as a second language. The Students who do not understand English cannot understand or sometimes read instructions. Classes such as US History will be a lot harder to understand if they do not know simple rules of the English language.

I look forward to improving my speaking and under- standing of English as it is vital for success in today's international world because I believe the international language is English.

Widad Salim
Africa

Me traslade a los Estados Unidos hace seis años. A mi llegada me encontré frustrada he insegura hacia mi falta de habilidad para comunicarme.

De un lugar donde mi trabajo como periodista requiere la constante exposición a las personas y la libre expresión de mis ideas y de repente no puede decir lo que pensaba era frustrante.

Por lo tanto, decidí inscribirme en el programa pa- ra adultos de ESL a fin de superar esta limitación, y

desde entonces mi vida ha cambiado por completo. He tenido la oportunidad de completar el programa y mi estatus en un año, a ser un ciudadano de los Estados, y ahora mantengo una posición de supervisora.

El impacto de ESL en mi vida es algo que puedo ver a diario en el trabajo, en casa y en las actividades sociales, mi vida es mucho más fácil y feliz porque pue- do expresar mis ideas con confianza.

He hecho nuevos amigos, soy capaz de viajar sin ninguna dificultad, y lo más importante es que soy capaz de comunicar mis ideas a los demás. Ya no me siento in- segura por el contrario me siento empoderada.

Gracias al programa de ESL estoy mejorando cada día y todo es más fácil en mi vida, estos programas ayudan a muchas personas como yo con deseos de superación, en lo particular yo recomiendo estos pro- gramas, ya que realmente si funcionan.

I moved to the United States six years ago. Upon my arrival, I found myself frustrated and insecure, due to my inability to communicate.

Coming from a place where my job as a journalist required constant exposure to people and free expression of ideas, and then all of a sudden not being able to say what I was thinking was quite frustrating.

I therefore decided to enroll in the English as a Second language at Central Texas College with the Adult Education Department in order to overcome this limitation; and since then my life has completely changed. I was able to complete the program in a year, become a United States Citizen, and now I hold a supervisory position.

The impact of ESL on my life is something that I can see on a daily basis, at work, at home, in social activities. My life is so much easier and joyful because I can express my ideas with some confidence.

I have made new friends, am able to travel without any difficulties, and most importantly, I am able to communicate my ideas to others. I no longer feel insecure. On the contrary, I feel empowered.

Thanks to ESL I'm getting better every day and everything is easier in my life. These programs help a lot of people like me, and I will recommend this program because it really works.

Roxidania Karron
Honduras

D.S-R

Acknowledge shortcomings
Believe in yourself
Curb your anger
Do your best at all times
Encourage yourself and others
Focus on Faith
Garner your thoughts
Hone your talents and skills
Imagine
Jubilate
Keep the Faith
Love your Lord
Mould minds

Nurture your self worth
Open your heart
Pray constantly
Query
Realize your dreams
Stay grounded
Talk to HIM
Understand your purpose
Volunteer your presence
Welcome each day
X out evil
Yearn to learn
Zap hatred

My thoughts on ESL

We can face many difficulties when we live as members of a different culture, in another country. "Language" is one of them.

In Korea, English education is focused on reading and grammar. We spend quite a long time in school learning English, but we don't have many opportunities to speak. So, we often experience limited conversations with Americans.

When I met other parents at my child's school, I couldn't continue the conversation after a simple greeting, and the embarrassment of finishing up with a smile led me to the English as a second language class. I thought that because of my lack of tenacity, I could study more efficiently than studying alone at home, and my ESL choice was not wrong.

When I first saw my teacher in class, she was very meticulous and strict. The class was well organized, and it included grammar, writing, and speaking and listening comprehension. Grammar textbooks and media were also used, and discussions were held using newspaper articles that were researched every week.

When there was a holiday, we could learn more about American culture or history by completing homework assignments and discussions.

My teacher also dealt with topics such as Civics and citizenship services, where we could acquire the basic knowledge we need to live in the United States.

What I thought was the most effective part of the class was "what I learned today". This was a task to say and write what we learned that day, so we had to pay attention and concentrate to be able to do it.

I think reviewing exercises can be a very effective way of learning for someone who is passionate, because they naturally study the parts they do not know during the review process.

Classes always passed without time to think about

anything else, and every time I came home with a lot of homework, I thought. "What should I do with all this homework"? "Can others do all this homework"?

Honestly, there were many moments when I wanted to give up while taking classes. There were many times when I didn't have time to prepare dinner because of the large amount of homework. Sometimes I had to sit at my desk when my child asked me to hug or play with her, and there were many times when I couldn't cook delicious food like before.

I had to give up many things such as tea time with my friends, shopping, watching interesting dramas, and naps... After putting my child to sleep at night, I looked for newspaper articles to take to class even if I was sleepy, and studied things I didn't know by asking my husband or child.

Sometimes I wondered if this much homework would really help. But I felt a slight change. Instead of short answers, YES or NO, I began to focus on making perfectly organized sentences and reading at least two newspaper articles and news stories every day.

I thought it was important to know what was going on where I lived, even if I didn't understand the article one hundred percent. This was a very positive change that I got from the class, as well as the improvement of my English skills.

Also, her class was a very good stimulus for me. I have never seen an educator so passionate and sincere. So, whenever I wanted to give up, I changed my mind when I thought about how precious it is to be able to take a class with a competent teacher.

Also, my teacher paid attention to and communicated with students' emotions as well as their studies and supported us when we were having a hard time emotionally.

There were many students from various countries in our class. My teacher gave a class that all students could identify with, understand and respect the culture of other countries.

Also, she actively explored the language of other

countries to recognize any similarities and differences with English, which was very admirable.

When my daughter's school was closed because of covid-19, I had no choice but to give up my class, and even then, my teacher encouraged me not to give up my homework online.

My experience in the past months has allowed me to make more natural English sentences, read English news articles like a habit, and have fun learning English. It was an honor to learn the foundation of language essential to life in America from my teacher.

In the past, I had taught Korean to children for a while. That's why I know how difficult it is to teach and understand someone, and how much responsibility it takes. So, I really appreciate what our teacher has done for us, and I want to express my respect and thanks to my husband and daughter for supporting and helping me.

Also, I would like to recommend our teacher's class confidently to students who are hesitating to apply for ESL classes somewhere.

Yukyung Jeon
Korea

ESL에 대한 나의 생각

우리는 태어난 곳과 다른 문화의 구성원으로 살아갈때 여러가지 어려움에 부딪힐 수 있다.

"언어" 또한 그 중 하나이다.

한국에서는 주로 독해와 문법 위주로 영어 교육이 이루어진다.

우리는 학창시절의 꽤 오랜시간을 영어를 배우는데에 투자하지만 막상 스피킹을 해볼 기회는 별로 없기에 미국인과의 대화에서 말문이 막히는것을 경험하게 된다.

내 아이의 학교에서 다른 학부모와 마주쳤을때, 간단한 안부인사 뒤로 대화를 이어가지 못하고, 미소로 마무리 짓고 돌아설때의 당혹감이 나를 ESL 수업으로 이끌었다.

의지가 약한 내 성격상 집에서 혼자 하는 공부 보다는 강제성이 있어야지만 보다 효율적인 공부가 될 수 있을 것이라 생각했고, 그 선택은 틀리지 않았다.

선생님을 수업에서 처음 보았을때 그녀는 아주 꼼꼼하고 무서운 인상이었다.

수업은 문법과 쓰기, 말하기와 듣기 등 어느 것 하나 빠지지 않고 짜임새 있게 운영되고 있었다. 문법 교재와 언론매체등도 활용되었고 매주 연구한 신문기사를 활용해 토론도 진행됐다.

기념일이 있을때에는 그것에 대해 조사하는 과제를 통해서 미국 문화나 역사에 대해 보다 정확히 알 수 있었다.

선생님은 시민권 취득등 우리가 미국생활을 하는데 필요한 기본적인 지식을 습득할 수 있는 주제도 다루어 주셨다.

내가 수업에서 가장 효과적이라고 생각했던 부분은 <what I learn today> 라는 과제였다.

이것은 오늘 무슨 내용을 배우고 느꼈는지 리뷰하는 과제였는데, 학생들이 수업시간에 주의를 기울이고 집중을 해야만 이 과제를 할 수 있다.

수업시간이 끝나면 모두 잊어 버리고 지나가는것이 아니라 과제를 통해서 스스로 다시 한번 복습을 하게되기 때문에 지식을 내것으로 만드는데에 큰 도움이 된다.

복습과정에서 자연스럽게 내가 모르는 부분을 더 탐구하게 되기때문에 이 과제는 누군가에겐 귀찮을 수 있지만 열의를 가진 누군가에겐 매우 효과적인 학습방법이 될수 있다고 생각한다.

수업은 언제나 잠시도 다른 생각을 할 겨를이 없이 시간이 흘러갔고, 숙제를 한가득 안고 집으로 돌아올 때마다 다는 생각했다.

"도대체 이 많은 숙제를 다 어떻게 해야 할까?" "다른 사람들은 이 숙제를 다 해낼 수 있을까?"

솔직히 수업을 들으면서도 나는 포기 하고 싶은 순간이 많았다.

과제의 양이 매우 많아 저녁을 준비 할 시간이 없을 때도 많았다. 때로는 아이가 안아달라, 놀아달라고 할 때에도 책상에 앉아야 했고, 예전처럼 맛있는 요리도 해주지 못할때가 많았다.

친구들과 가지던 티 타임, 쇼핑, 재미있는 드라마 시청, 여유로운 낮잠등
많은 것을 포기할수 밖에 없었다. 밤에 아이를 재우고 나서 잠이 쏟아져도 수업에 가져갈 신문기사를 찾아보고 모르는 것들은 남편이나 아이에게 물어보면서 공부했다.

때로는 이 많은 숙제가 과연 도움이 되는것일까 하는 생각이 들었다. 그러나 나는 조금씩 변화를 느꼈다. 단답형 YES or NO 대신 완벽한 형태를
갖춘 문장을 만드는것에 집중하기 시작했고 과제가 아니어도 매일 신문기사나 뉴스를 최소한 5개이상 읽었다.

기사를 백프로 이해하지 못하더라도 내가 사는곳에 무슨 일이 일어나고
있는지 아는것이 중요하다는 생각이 들었기 때문이다. 이는 영어 실력
향상 이외에도 수업이 나에게 가져다 준 매우 긍정적인 변화였다.

또한 그녀의 수업은 나에게 아주 좋은 자극제였다. 나는 지금까지 그녀만큼 열정적이고 성실한 교육자를 보지 못했다. 그래서 포기하고 싶을때마다 내가 유능한 선생님의 강의를 들을 수 있다는것이 얼마나 소중한 기회인가 생각하며 마음을 고쳐 먹었다.

또한 선생님께서는 학업 뿐만 아니라 학생들의 감정에도 주목하고 소통하며 우리가 정서적으로 힘들때도 지지해 주셨다.

D.S-R

우리 수업에는 다양한 나라에서 온 학생들이 많았다. 선생님께서는 모든 학생들이 다른 나라의 문화를 이해하고 존중 하면서 공감 할 수 있는 수업을 하셨다.

또 선생님께서 다른 나라의 언어에 관심이 많으셔서 각 나라의 말이 영어와 어떤점이 비슷하고 다른지 적극적으로 탐구하는 모습도 매우 존경스러웠다.

Covid-09로 인해 내 아이의 학교가 문을 닫았을때 나는 수업을 포기할
수 밖에 없었고 그 때에도 선생님께서는 온라인으로 과제를 내 주시며
끝까지 포기하지 않도록 격려해 주셨다.

지난 몇개월 간의 경험으로 인해 나는 보다 자연스러운 영어 문장을 만들 수 있게 되었고, 습관처럼 영어 뉴스 기사를 읽어보게 되었으며. 영어를 배우는것에 즐거움을 느끼게 되었다. 내가 선생님으로부터 미국
생활에 필수적인 언어의 기초를 배울 수 있었던 것은 매우 영광이었다.

과거 나는 잠시동안 아이들을 상대로 한국어 교육을 해 본 적이 있었다. 그렇기 때문에 누군가를 가르치고 이해시키는 행위가 얼마나 어려운 것인지, 얼마나 책임감이 따르는 행위인지를 잘 알고 있다. 그래서
선생님께서 우리에게 해 주신 일에 정말 감사하고, 존경을 표하고 싶다.

그리고 내가 공부할 수 있도록 나를 지지해 주고 도와준 남편과 딸아이에게 고마움을 전하며,

어딘가에서 ESL수업 신청을 망설이고 있을 학생들에게 우리 선생님의
수업을 자신있게 추천 해주고 싶다.

전 유 경.

MY EXPERIENCE IN ESL CLASS

My first ESL class in the United States of America was at Central Texas College on Ft. Hood, Texas. I found it compelling and engaging. I met a lot people of different nationalities and cultures.

Our class was not only about English as a Second Language, but also about American history, national celebrations, and customs. Every evening we had homework assignments, which sometimes were a lot, but they helped us to practice our spelling, writing and to think in English.

The class was never boring, and we learned in different ways, by speaking, writing, watching movies, and writing essays about the movies. I liked the fact that we could "play teacher "by giving our peers spelling words and correcting them.

Extra motivation was "ESL Class Dollars". Sometimes when we answered certain questions correctly, or if we had perfect attendance for the week, we would receive the ESL dollars. We would be able to spend those dollars at an ESL Shopping Spree at the end of the year.

We also cherished each other's culture and customs. By sharing our different lifestyles, customs and food, we could understand, learn from each other and appreciate each other. One special event for us was an International Potluck on Christmas or Thanksgiving.

The class was interesting, still very respectful, and educational.

Ilva Rivera
Latvia

Mana pieredze mācoties angļu valodu kā svešvalodu Amerikā

Šī bija mana pirmā Anglu valodas klase Amerikas Savienotajās Valstīs, kas notika Centrālās Teksasas koledžā, Fort Hood Teksasā. Es satiku daudzus dažādu tautību cilvēkus. Mūsu studās mēs mācījāmies ne tikai angļu valodu kā otro svešvalodu, bet arī Amerikas vēsturi, nacionālas svinības un paražas. Katru vakaru mums bija mājasdarbi, kuri dažkārt bija diezgan daudz, bet tie palīdzēja trenēt pareizrakstību un domāt angļu valodā. Angļu valodas stundas nekad nebija garlaicīgas, mēs mācijāmies anglu valodu runājot, rakstot, skatoties filmas, un rakstot esejas par filmu. Mēs varējam spēlēt skolotāju, diktējot skolniekiem vārdus, lai trenētu pareizrakstību un vēlak tos laboot. Papildus motivācija skolniekiem, bija atbildēt pareizi uz skolotājas jautājumiem, lai nopelnītu klases naudu, ko mēs varējam iztērēt gada beigās. Iepazīstoties un uzzinot dažādus dzīvesveidus, paražas un ēdiena atšķirības, mūs iemācija novērtēt katra īpašo vērtību. Lielākais prieks bija svinēt visiem kopā Ziemassvētkus un Pateicības dienu, uzcienājot viens otru ar ipašo nacionālo ēdienu.

Stundas bija interesantas, cieņpilnas un izglītojošas.

Ilva Rivera
Latvia

"Education due to lockdown"

The first half of 2020 was difficult for all of us. People around the world were challenged to leave their comfort zone and do something different. One of the areas that suffered was education. Three categories of people in that area suffered due to lockdown: children/students, teachers and parents. Nobody was prepared for the lockdown, but fortunately people quickly found solutions for that problem.

The remote learning was an excellent idea in the beginning, but after some time, I found out that it wasn't so good. I think so, because nobody was prepared for the lockdown, and some teachers didn't know how to manage distance learning. It is not their fault, and all of them did an extraordinary job. They adapted quickly to a new situation and continued to teach children and students even though it was not easy.

On the other hand, some children were at home with their parents. For them it also wasn't easy. Parents were challenged to work from home while their children were homeschooled.

I thought about families who have two or more children who have to be schooled at home. I think it was extremely hard for them to balance work and kids at the same time.

This lockdown created a short and long-term issue. The severe short-term disruption is felt by families around the world. Home schooling is not only a massive shock to parents' productivity, but also to children's social life and learning.

Students' assessments were continued online, with a lot of trial and error and uncertainty for everyone. Many assessments have been canceled. More important, these interruptions will not just be a short-term issue, but can also be a long term consequence for the affected cohorts and are likely to increase inequality[1].

Even though there is still the pandemic, most schools, colleges and universities are going to reopen this fall. Texas public schools will be required to provide in-person instructions for students this fall. There are mandatory safety precautions such as staff and students wearing masks, sanitizing their hands regularly and staying 6 feet away from one another[2].

There is still a high risk, and there will be a lot of new cases of infection with the coronavirus.Despite this, I believe that we must continue to learn either from a distance or face-to-face, because education plays an important role in our lives.

1. https://voxeu.org/article/impact-covid-19-education
2. https://www.texastribune.org/2020/06/23/texas-planning-few-mandatory-safety-measures-when-schools-reopen-draft/

Eleonora Onofrei
Moldova

"Educația pe timp de carantină"

Prima jumătate al anului 2020 a fost dificilă pentru noi toți. Oamenii din întreaga lume au fost provocați să-și părăsească zona de confort și să facă ceva diferit. Una dintre ariile care a avut de suferit a fost educația. Trei categorii de persoane din aceasta arie au suferit în timpul carantinei: copii/studenții, profesorii și părinții. Nimeni nu era pregătit pentru această carantină, însă din fericire oamenii au găsit rapid soluții pentru această problemă.

Învățarea de la distanță a fost o idee excelenta la început, însă după ceva timp mi-am dat seama că nu a fost atât de bună. Cred asta, deoarece, nimeni nu era pregătit pentru carantină și mulți profesori nu știau cum să dirijeze învățarea de la distanță. Aceata nu este greșeala lor, toți profesorii au făcut un lucru extraordinar. Ei rapid s-au adaptat la situația nouă și au continuat sa învețe copii și studenții chiar dacă nu era deloc ușor.

De cealaltă parte, unii copii erau acasă cu părinții lor. Pentru ei aceasta tot nu a fost ușor. Părinții au fost provocați să lucreze de acasă în timp ce copiii învățau de acasă.

Mă gândeam la familiile care au doi sau mai mulți copii și care învățau de acasă. Mă gândesc ca a fost extrem de greu pentru părinți să balanseze serviciul și grija de copii în același timp.

Acestă carantină a creat probleme de termen scurt și lung. Perturbările pe termen scurt sunt simțite de familii din întreaga lume. Învățatul de acasă nu este un șoc doar pentru productivitatea părinților, dar și pentru viața socială și învățământul copiilor. Evaluarea studenților a continuat online cu o mulțime de procese, erori și incertitudini pentru fiecare. Multe evaluări au fost anulate. Cel mai important este faptul ca aceste întreruperi vor provoca nu numai probleme de scurta durată, dar vor avea consecințe pe termen lung pentru cohortele afectate și prin urmare sunt susceptibile să crească inegalitatea[1].

Chiar dacă încă ne aflam în pandemie, majoritatea școlilor, colegiilor și universităților se vor redeschide la toamnă. Școlile publice din Texas vor trebui să furnizeze instrucțiuni în persoană pentru studenți in această toamnă. Există câteva precauții obligatorii de siguranță ca și purtarea măștilor de către studenți și personal, dezinfectarea regulată a mâinilor și păstrarea distantei de 6 feet dintre oameni[2].

Încă există un risc înalt de îmbolnăvire, și vor fi încă multe cazuri noi de infecție cu Coronavirus. În pofida acestui fapt, eu consider că noi trebuie sa continuăm să învățăm fie de la distanță sau față-în-față, deoarece educația are un rol important în viața noastră.

"April 7, 2009"

I remember an incident that happened in my country. That incident changed the history of Moldova. Until April 2009, in Moldova the majority of seats in parliament were communists, and the country was considered a communist country.

A lot of people hoped that after the election something will change, but the reality was different. People started a protest after the announcement of preliminary election results on April 6, 2009, which showed the Party of Communists of the Republic of Moldova winning approximately 50% of the votes. Another reason for the protest was that the democrats claimed that the elections have been forged.

The protest started in two cities, in Chișinău the number of protesters was approximately 30,000, and in Bălți, the number was above 7,000. Most of them were students and young people. The protests were peaceful at the beginning, but on April 7, the demonstrations turned into a riot. Rioters attacked the parliament building and presidential office, breaking windows, setting furniture on fire and stealing property.

The protest against the election turned into conflict with the police, who used tear gas and water cannons. Unfortunately, there were a lot of people who were injured, four people died and about 300 participants were arrested. After that the protests were peaceful until April 15,2009.

April 7, 2009 will remain an important day in the history of my country. Students and young people fought for justice and died for it.

Eleonora Onofrei
Moldova

"7 Aprilie 2009"

Îmi amintesc un incident care s-a întâmplat în țara mea. Acest incident a schimbat istoria Moldovei. Până în Aprilie 2009, în Moldova majoritatea scaunelor din parlament erau ocupate de comuniști, și țara era considerată o țară comunistă.

Mulți oameni au sperat că după alegeri situația se va schimba, însă realitatea era alta. Oamenii au început să protesteze după anunțarea rezultatelor preliminare din 6 Aprilie 2009, care arătau că Particul Comunist din Republica Moldova au câștigat aproximativ 50% din voturi.

Un alt motiv pentru protest a fost faptul că democrații au cerut revindecarea voturilor din cauza că alegerile au fost fraudate.

Protestele au început în două orașe, în Chișinău numarul protestatarilor era de 30,000, iar în Bălți numărul era de aproape 7,000. Majoritatea protestatarilor erau studenți și tineri. Protestele erau pașnice la început, însă pe 7 Aprilie, demonstrațiile s-au transformat într-o rascoală. Protestatarii au atacat clădirea parlamentului și oficiul prezidențial, stricând geamurile, dând foc mobilierului și furând din oficii.

Protestele împotriva alegerilor s-a transformat într-un conflict dintre protestatari și poliție, care utiliza gaz lacrimogen și furtunuri cu apă.

Din nefericire, au fost foarte mulți oameni care au fost răniți, patru persoane au decedat, iar peste 300 de participanți au fost arestați. După aceasta, protestele au fost pașnice până pe data de 15 Aprilie 2009.

Data de 7 Aprilie 2009 va rămâne o zi importantă în istoria țării mele. Studenții și tinerii au luptat pentru justiție și au murit pentru ea.

Eleonora Onofrei
Moldova

"My English as a Second Language Class Experience"

For me, as an immigrant, the English as a second language class was a good start in my new life in the United States. This class gives many opportunities for students and teaches them a lot of things.

First of all, I'm not afraid anymore to speak English with native speakers. Even though I make mistakes, people understand me, and I understand them. That happens because in the English as a Second language class, we all are immigrants, and all of us speak different languages.

Secondly, I have met new people from different countries and learned about different cultures. I made new friends and I think that is the most important thing. Now, I have people I can communicate with here in the United States. The ESL class gives me the possibility of forming new relationships.

I thank my teacher for her time and dedication. I am happy I am in this class. I have met a lot of people and learn new things. Besides that, I learned about the country where I live now. I learned about the opportunities in the United States, and of course, I learned English.

Eleonora Onofrei
Moldova

"Experiența mea în clasa Engleza ca a doua limbă"

Pentru mine ca emigrant, clasa Engleza ca a doua limbă a fost un bun început pentru noua mea viața în Statele Unite ale Americii. Aceată clasa oferă oportunități pentru studenți și îi învață multe lucruri.

Mai întâi de toate, deja nu mai am frica să vorbesc cu nativii vorbitori de Engleză. Chiar dacă mai fac unele greșeli, oamenii mă înțeleg și eu îi înțeleg pe ei. Aceasta s-a întâmplat datorită clasei ESL, deoarece acolo eram toți emigranți și toți vorbeam diferite limbi.

În al doilea rând, am întîlnit oamenii noi din diferite țări și am învățat despre diferite culturi. Mi-am făcut prieteni noi, și cred că acesta e cel mai important lucru. Acum am oameni cu care pot să comunic și să mă întâlnesc, aici, în Statele Unite. Posibilitatea de a forma noi relații, aceasta e ceea ce mi-a oferit clasa ESL.

Îi mulțumesc profesoarei mele pentru timpul și dedicația ei. Sunt fericită că sunt în această clasă. Am întîlnit oamenii noi și am învățat diferite lucruri. Pe lângă toate astea, am învățat despre țara în care trăiesc acum. Am învățat despre oportunitățile care sunt în Statele Unite, și desigur limba Engleză.

Eleonora Onofrei
Moldova

SUGGESTIONS FROM A FORMER ESL STUDENT

My name is Liseth Valbuena, and I'm from Venezuela. I'm married to an American soldier, and that is the reason why I had to move to the United States (of America).

When I came to this country I knew that I had to learn English, because I didn't want to depend on my husband all the time because I didn't know how to speak English.

I decided to start this course, and now after about nine months, I can tell you that I completed my ESL course and I feel really satisfied and proud of myself.

From the beginning, I put all my energy and dedication into it, because learning another language is not easy. You have to have a real desire to learn. If you come to class only to spend some hours here or because your husband wants it, then you will waste your time.

I have to tell you that this course is not easy, not only because you have to study all the lessons, but also because you must come to class almost four hours a day, five days a week.

In my case, maybe it seems easier for me to other people because I don't have children. But I had plenty of activities to do, besides the class, that occupied my time too. Plus, I don't have my own car, and sometimes it was hard too. But I did it, and you will do it too.

Sometimes you have an appointment, or maybe you or your children will feel sick, but those are eventualities. Please don't invent fake excuses to avoid coming to class. Remember that while you are in this course, there are many people outside who want to be in your place in this classroom.

When my teacher asked me if I could write a letter telling you all my experience in this course, of course I said yes. We think that if a student like me, who already finished the course from the beginning, tells you what to expect, what to do, what things worked for me, and other things based on my own experience, maybe it will help you to achieve your own goal.

The first thing I want to tell you is not to be scared to ask questions, and don't be scared to make mistakes. Remember that this is not your native language, and each time you have an error the teacher is going to correct you, and you won't see any progress if you are a passive student instead of an active one.

Maybe you think that you are learning when you are paying attention to the other students' doubts, and that is true, but remember, those are their mistakes, not yours, and maybe you will forget the explanation the teacher will give to correct them faster than the explanation to correct your own mistakes.

Another important thing you must do is do your homework every day, even though you think it is not necessary or it is hard, because if the teacher asks you to do something it is because she knows you can do it, and most importantly, she knows you need to do it. But if you really want to improve, do your homework by yourself.

Try to review your classes every now and then, because if you don't understand one lesson perhaps you will not understand the next one.

Try to be always on time for class, not only because maybe you will miss something important, but also because when you come late you cause distraction and noise, and sometimes the other students can't concentrate. Think that this is not a joke or a game; this is a very serious thing to everybody.

In my case I preferred to sit in the front seats of the classroom because in the majority of times, people who want to talk more are the people who are seated in the back rows, especially on the first days.

Sometimes people take the back places because they think that the teacher is not aware that they are there... don't even think about it. Our teacher is going to learn your names the first day of the class and she will ask questions to everybody, no matter where they are seated.

It's preferable if you sit with a partner who doesn't speak your language. That helps you to speak in English if you want to communicate with him or her.

When you have some discussions in class about any topic, don't be afraid to say whatever is on your mind; simply try to explain your thoughts in the best way that you can, and trust me... little by little you will be better and better each time.

Keep your notes, exercises, homework, etc... in a folder. Don't throw away the papers you use here, because you never know when the teacher will ask for something. Take notes in the class even though you don't understand at that moment. You have to study by yourselves at home.

Don't limit your English studies only to this class. The teacher is going to give you the basics but you have to investigate more if you want to improve faster.

In our ESL classes we received visits from some guest speakers who talked about different topics. It was interesting because sometimes you have a problem and you don't know what to do, and those people can help you.

One of the things I enjoyed more was when we watched movies. After that, we had discussions about them or sometimes we had to write what the movie was about. It was a big challenge for me, because when I started I couldn't write more than one page, and with a lot of mistakes. But at the end I could write many pages, plenty of mistakes too but in a less quantity. It could happen to you too, if you will not be afraid to write, and make all your corrections.

In my experience, I really enjoyed our field trips, to the Planetarium, to the Central Texas College Campus Tours and to the City Hall in Killeen. Each time I learned different things that maybe many people who have been here in Killeen for many years don't know yet. You have that opportunity, and also it will be free. Don't waste your time; ask questions, be interested, and try to listen and understand what the people in those places say to you.

Remember, your ears will be accustomed to hear how the teacher speaks. You have to listen and understand when other people are talking. Maybe it will be a hard time for many of you, but don't worry about it; you are not the only one. That still happened to me too sometimes.

One of the biggest challenges for me was when we had to create a business project. We had to act and speak (in English) in front of an audience, different from our classmates and our teacher. Even though we were afraid, we did it very well.

At the end of the course, please don't expect that you are going to speak as people who have been here for many years, but certainly you are going to be able to maintain a normal conversation at the hospital, in the bank, in the supermarket, and also many of you will be ready to attend college.

Some days maybe you will feel that you are not learning enough, but let me tell you once again trust me, don't feel frustrated, you are going to make it. Suddenly you will speak English, and you will not even know when it happened. Of course, you need more than nine months to speak very well, but this is the beginning.

I can write ten more pages telling you what to do or what not to do based on my experience, but I think that each person is different. But it will work for everybody if you have the real desire the constant dedication, and the strong determination to do it.

Live your own experience as best as you can. I hope that you will enjoy and take advantage of this course as I did.

One last thing, please, please, pleeeaaaseee if some day you can't attend the class please call teacher or at least send her a message, but don't forget to write your name on it.

P.S. Maybe some of you would like to know who the teacher is, but I can't tell you anything, because our teacher doesn't like to hear compliments from us to her. All I have to say about her are good things; she is one of the best teachers I have ever had.

Liseth Valbuena
Venezuela

MI EXPERIENCIA COMO ESTUDIANTE DE INGLES COMO SEGUNDA LENGUA (ESL).

Mi nombre es Liseth Valbuena y soy de Venezuela. Estoy casada con un soldado Americano y esa es la razón por la cual me tuve que mudar a los Estados Unidos de América.

Desde que vine a este país, yo sabía que tenía que aprender Inglés porque no quería depender de mi esposo todo el tiempo por no saber como hablarlo.

Decidí empezar este curso, y ahora despues de alrededor de nueve meses puedo decirles que completé mi curso de ESL y me siento realmente satisfecha y orgullosa de mí. Desde el principio puse todas mis energías y dedicación en esto, porque aprender otro idioma no es fácil. Hay que tener el verdadero deseo de apren- der. Si vienen a clase solo para pasar algunas horas aca o porque sus esposos(as) así lo quieren, pues entonces perderán el tiempo.

Tengo que decirles que este curso no es fácil, no solo porque tienen que estudiar todas las lecciones, sino porque deben venir a clases de casi cuatro horas al día, cinco veces a la semana.

En mi caso quizás pareciera ser más fácil que para otras personas, porque no tengo hijos. Pero yo tuve muchas otras actividades que hacer además de las clases, que también ocuparon mi tiempo. Además, yo no tengo mi carro propio y muchas veces eso fué difícil también. Pero lo hice, y tu tambien lo haras.

Algunas veces tendrán una cita, o quizás ustedes o sus hijos se enfermarán, pero esas son eventualidades. Por favor, no inventen falsas excusas para no venir a clases. Recuerden que mientras ustedes están en este curso, hay muchas personas afuera que quisieran estar en sus puestos en este salón de clases.

Cuando mi profesor me pidió que si podría escribir una

carta contándoles a ustedes como fué toda mi experiencia en este curso, por supuesto que dije que si. Nosotras pensamos que sí algún estudiante como yo, que ya terminé el curso complete desde el principio, les dijera que esperar, que hacer, que cosas funcionaron en mí, y otras cosas más basadas en mi propia experiencia, quizás eso les ayudará a ustedes a lograr su objetivo.

La primera cosa que les quiero decir es que no teman hacer preguntas, ni teman cometer errores. Recuerden que éste no es su idioma natal, y además cada vez que cometan un error, la profesora les corregirá, y nunca verán ningún progreso si son un estudiante pasivo en vez de uno activo.

Quizás piensen que están aprendiendo cuando prestan atención a las dudas de otros estudiantes, y es cierto, pero recuerden, esas son las dudas de ellos, no las de ustedes, y tal vez olvidarán la explicación que la profesora dará para corregirlos a ellos, más rápido que la explicación que ella dará para corregir sus propios errores.

Otra cosa importante es que deben hacer sus tareas todos los días, a pesar de que piensen que no es necesario o piensen que es difícil, porque sí la profesora les pide hacer algo es porque ella sabe que lo pueden hacer, y más importante es, que ella sabe que ustedes necesitan hacerlo. Pero, sí realmente quieren mejorar, hagan sus tareas ustedes mismos.

Traten de repasar sus clases de vez en cuando, porque sí no entienden una lección quizás no entenderán la próxima. Traten de estar siempre puntuales en la clase, no solo porque se pueden perder de algo importante, sino porque cuando llegan tarde causan distracción y ruido y algunas veces los otros estudiantes no pueden estar concentrados debido a eso. Piensen que esto no es una broma, o un juego, esto es algo muy serio para todos.

En mi caso, yo prefer sentarme en las filas de alante del salon de clase, porque no siempre, pero si en la mayoría de los casos, la gente que quiere estar hablando se sienta en las filas de atrás, especialmente los primeros días.

Muchas veces la gente se sienta atrás porque piensan que la profesora no está consciente de que están allí...ni siquiera piensen en eso. Nuestra profesora se aprenderá todos sus nombres el primer día de clases y hará preguntas a todo el mundo, sin importer donde estén sentados. Es preferable si se sientan con una pareja que no hable su mismo idioma. Eso ayuda a hablar Inglés, sí se quieren comunicar con él o ella.

Cuando hay alguna discussion en clase sobre algún tópico, no teman decir lo que sea que se les venga a la mente, simplemente traten de explicar sus pensamientos de la mejor manera que puedan, y creanme...poco a poco estarán mejor y mejor cada vez.

Mantengan sus notas, ejercicios, tareas, etc, en una carpeta. No tiren los papeles que usan acá, porque ustedes nunca sabrán cuando la profesora pedirá algo.

Tomen notas de la clase así no entiendan nada en el momento. Tienen que estudiar por su cuenta en la casa. No limíten sus estudios de Inglés solo a esta clase. La profesora les dará lo básico pero ustedes tienen que investigar más sí quieren progresar más rápido.

En nuestras clases de ESL nosotros recibimos la visita de algunos oradores invitados que nos hablaron de diferentes temas. Fué interesante porque algunas veces tenemos algún problema y no sabemos que hacer, y esas personas quizás pueden ayudarnos.

Una de las cosas que yo disfruté más fué cuando veíamos películas. Después de verlas teníamos discusiones acerca de las mismas y a veces teníamos que escribir de qué trataba la película.

Fué un gran reto para mí porque cuando empecé yo no

podía escribir más de una hoja, y con muchos errores. Pero al final del curso pude escribir muchas páginas, con muchos errores también, pero menos que antes. Eso les podría pasar a ustedes también sí no tienen miedo de escribir y si hacen todas las correcciones que la profesora les haga.

En mi experiencia, yo realmente disfruté nuestros paseos fuera del salon de clases, al Planetario, a el Tour por el campus de CTC y al Ayuntamiento o Municipio de Killeen. Cada vez aprendí cosas diferentes que quizás mucha gente que ha vivido aca en Killeen por muchos años, no conoce aún. No desperdicien su tiempo alli, hagan preguntas, muestren interés y traten de escuchar y entender lo que la gen- te en esos sitios les están diciendo.

Recuerden que sus oídos estarán acostumbrados a escuchar como habla la profesora. Tienen que escuchar y entender cuando les hablan otras personas, quizás sera difícil para muchos de ustedes, pero no se preocupen, ustedes no son los únicos. Eso me sigue pasando a mí algunas veces.

Uno de los retos más grandes para mí fué cuando tuvimos que crear un proyecto de negocio. Tuvimos que actuar y hablar en frente de una audiencia, diferente a nuestros compañeros de clase y a nuestra profesora. A pesar de que estuvimos asustados, lo hicimos bastante bien.

Al final del curso, por favor no esperen que van a hablar inglés como la gente que ha estado acá por muchos años, pero ciertamente serán capaces de mantener una conversación normal en el hospital, en el banco, en el supermercado y también muchos de ustedes estarán listos para ir a la Universidad.

Algunos días quizás se sentirán que no están aprendiendo suficiente, pero dejenme decirles una vez más, créanme, no se sientan frustrados, lo van a lograr. De repente hablarán inglés y ni siquiera se darán cuenta cuando pasó. Por supuesto, se necesitan más de nueve meses para hablarlo muy bien, pero éste es el comienzo.

Podría escribir diez hojas mas diciéndoles que hacer o que no hacer basado en mi experiencia, pero creo que cada persona es diferente. Pero el curso funcionará en todos sí se tiene el deseo real, la constante dedicación y la fuerte determinación de hacerlo.

Vivan su propia experiencia lo major quepuedan. Espero que disfruten y aprovechen éste curso tanto como yo lo híce.

Una última cosa, por favor, por favor, por favoooooooor, sí algún día no pueden venir a clases, por favor llamen a la profesora o al menos envíenle un mensaje, pero no olviden escribir sus nombres en él.

P.D. Quizás muchos de ustedes quisieran saber como es la profesora, pero no puedo decirles nada, porque a nuestra profesora no le gusta escuchar halagos de nosotros hacia ella. Todo lo que tengo que decir acerca de ella son cosas buenas, …ella es una de las mejores profesoras que he tenido.

Liseth Valbuena
Venezuela

Human behavior is just as complicated as it is unpredictable because of the multitude of factors that exert influence over its very existence. While it is extremely important to examine these factors through dialogue and critical analysis, one cannot help but acknowledge the futility that often accompanies such exercises when it comes to reaching consensus on difficult issues like the management of two current viruses: One chronic systemic racism, and the other, Covid-19 which is relatively acute.

In both instances, there is so much that is known and unknown as evidenced by an almost insurmountable slew of questionable information coming from traditional media in general and social media in particular, that we often find ourselves in a conundrum as to what to believe.

Political affiliations and our personal subjective perceptions do not help our need for true enlightenment either, and as a result, we tend to cling to the strongholds that make us feel both comfortable and safe.

It is against this background one may want to consider focusing on the big picture rather than the myriad of positive and negative examples that can be quoted for or against our often-contrasting opinions, which once again, though highly interesting and useful, may not be necessarily solution-oriented. In other words, we may get caught up in the weeds at the expense of getting to the real root of the problem.

For example, we could argue ad infinitum about how the Coronavirus originated and who is to blame rather than take the necessary established measures to limit the spread and save lives, while a treatment/vaccine is being developed. Or, we could complain over and over again about police violence/brutality and not institute reform mechanisms that would help change undesirable practices.

We could also blame some people of color for their own "undesirable attitudes" instead of finding meaningful ways to reach such individuals through educational, spiritual and social development. None of these is easy, but they are practical tools that could help prevent us going round in circles again and again.

This is where it becomes tricky: In both cases there has to be "buy in" by all parties involved in order to be successful. However, the forest speaks one undeniable truth and that is....... whenever one group believes that it is superior to another group for any reason whatsoever, and it has the socioeconomic and military advantage over the other group, it is more likely to want to remain entrenched in that power unless there is some overriding benefit that can be accrued.

In fact, such a group will always operate in such a way to enhance and secure that status quo. Discrimination in all forms and at every level is a dangerous and desensitizing weapon that scars human beings for generations.

But we are all endowed with a conscience, and the way we treat others really does not have anything to do with our education because we instinctively know right from wrong in most cases. We may choose to practice willful ignorance or indulge in conscientious stupidity when it suits us, but the truth always convicts us in our hearts and minds. Or we may just not care!

Do you think the benefit might simply be just doing the right thing as God expects of all of us?

DRS

AFTERWORD

This is an inspiring book of how great people from other countries come together with a common purpose towards advancing in life and fulfilling their dreams.

The author has a way of empowering and encouraging others who may face obstacles in their lives, and she does it through her life of service. She not only lives a life of service, but also encourages others to give back through their volunteer efforts, care and concern as evidenced in this book.

This is a poetic book of positive stories as told by her and some of her great students. It is a book of positive mindset beliefs and inspiration as seen through the eyes of her wonderful heart, and some of the people who have had the pleasure of meeting her. Her book reveals the love and intense desire she has for teaching and writing, as illustrated in some of the numerous poems and articles she has written over the years.

Her students have witnessed and testified to her patience and her ability to listen, understand, sympathise and empathise. They are able to appreciate her with a degree of confidence and comfort allowing them to unfold some of their innermost thoughts and experiences.

I am indeed blessed to be able to say that I know someone like Dianna who makes a positive difference in people's lives, so they can in turn make a positive difference in our communities, as they continue on their own personal journey. Thank you Dianna for what you do to improve our communities. This is an absolutely uplifting book.

Jose Segarra
Mayor, Killeen, TX

ABOUT THE AUTHOR

A native of Port-of-Spain, Trinidad and Tobago, the author is a Multi-Level English as a Second Language (ESL) Instructor at Central Texas College, Fort Hood, TX., and has more than two decades of experience in writing, editing and teaching. She was a journalist and editor for various military newspapers in the United States and Berlin, Germany. She was a journalism instructor at the Defense Information School, Fort Benjamin Harrison, Ind. and at Fort Meade, Maryland, and rewrote and revitalized the Newswriting Programmed Instruction Book for the Basic Journalist Course. The author was a narrator and editor with the Public Affairs Office, First Cavalry Division, Fort Hood, Texas, and as Public Affairs Chief, wrote speeches for the command group. She is familiar with several languages and graduated in the top ten percent of the Russian Language Course at the Defense language Institute, DLI, Monterey, California. She has written poems, in brochure format and articles for Civilian and military newspapers in the U.S and Berlin, Germany. Her first book, with students' accounts, written in English and their native languages, and published in 2015, is a fascinating window into the experiences of immigrant students, from one dozen countries, studying ESL on Fort Hood, TX. Her third book "Barriers beyond Borders" is a thought provoking insight into her life, and the lives of some students, as immigrants residing in the United States. Coming soon!

Printed in the United States
by Baker & Taylor Publisher Services